Leave Your Life Alone

Leave You

by

 TEMPLEGATE, Publishe

Life Alone

Hubert van Zeller

Springfield, Illinois

© 1972 by Hubert van Zeller
All rights reserved
Library of Congress Catalog Card Number 72-78934
SBN 87243-043-X
Printed in the United States of America

FOR CLAUDIA AND CY
IN MEMORY OF KEVIN

"From the reality of the man who moulds his own life into completeness, it is only one step into egocentric isolation."

– Karl Jaspers

"The systematic cultivation of self-awareness may as easily produce undesirable as desirable results. Where personality is developed for its own sake, and not in order that it may be transcended, there tends to be a rising of the barriers of separateness and an increase of egotism."

– Aldous Huxley

Contents

1

Why?

Religion has to do with life and with self. So in a society which tests every aspect of life, and which is increasingly given to self-questioning, religion becomes more and more complicated. In the belief that by holding up traditionally accepted religious assumptions to the light of reason and re-examination they are bringing a greater simplicity into man's relations with God, with the world and with himself, modern thinkers are multiplying perplexities instead of solving them. Life is not meant to be lived in a test-tube or under X-ray. It is significant that to test the health of an organism beyond a certain point can produce the disease which the test was designed to obviate. Beyond a certain point religion can become so artificially cultured as to work against its own purposes. The culture can become a self-consuming growth. If religion is allowed to develop according to grace, and not always with one eye on the charts, it can be relied upon to give direction to life and self. Understandably the man without a clearly defined creed approaches the whole question of religion bewildered, bemused, sceptical and cynical. Where at one time a man used to regard religion as security, if not for himself at least for other people, now he regards it as sickness. Much of the blame for this must lie with those thinkers who, in their endeavour to open up the mind to an awareness of hitherto undiscovered realities, have succeeded in enclosing the mind within itself where there is room only to doubt the old realities.

If religion has been getting a bad name it is not because the Christian gospel is no longer able to do its work in the twentieth century, but because the exponents of Christianity have made such a science of religion that twentieth century man, looking for the simplicity of the gospel as Christ preached it, is put off. Twentieth century man can get what he wants, or thinks he can, from other gospels. If the searcher after truth sees Christians to be just as self-absorbed, guilt-ridden, unsure of their foundations, haunted by the same fears as he is, just as much at sea in an alien environment and just as psychotic generally as he himself is, it is hardly to be wondered at that he feels no attraction to the church. "If their Christian faith has got them no farther than that" he says, "then give me a religion which looks out instead of in." It should be one of our Christian convictions that introversion is the enemy of sanctification. Though religion is something more than an antidote to psychotic disorders, the fact that religious people are as mixed up as any obscures the real issue which is the love of God and love of neighbour.

Why?

Introspection is no new phenomenon in the history of religion. The Book of Job would suggest that holy men were liable to examine too closely their motives, mistakes, aspirations and frustrations, and that amateur psychologists were not wanting who were only too ready to probe into causes and to proffer reasoned, analytical, and for the most part idiotic, advice. Many of the psalms, too, are in the form of painful self-searching. But whereas the tendency has hitherto been looked upon as something to be watched and disciplined, today it is looked upon almost as something to be proud of. Once a hazard to be corrected – and one which can be turned to good use as this book will attempt to show – soul-screening has been so exaggerated as to become in many cases obsessive. As in the case of many disorders, the sufferers can derive great satisfaction from being victims of it. Everybody's nerve-ends are, as the result of both personal and collective self-recrimination, so sensitive that to read or hear or see anything which has to do with the contemporary scene sets off an alarm bell. At once our share, blown up beyond reason, in the injustices of the world is brought home to us: we feel guiltily responsible. We cast about for evidence, for reassurance, for excuse. What we fail to realize is that by exposing too much we end up unable to experience. By plotting our reactions too minutely we end up unable to feel them. This might in one way be an advantage – we would pay less attention to them – but on the other hand we would lose in the quality of human compassion. A better course would be to forget about our reactions and to think about other people's. Inevitably we learn from ourselves, but this should not be an end in itself. We profit from our learning by forgetting about our learning. We are only the book of reference, not the book of study. It is the same in the case of prayer — we may use the classical methods, not in order to fulfill a set of instructions but in order to do without them eventually.

Religious people, perhaps because more than most they are afraid of missing a signpost, are apt to take up one recommendation after another, applying them scrupulously but without reference to the scene as a whole. "Know thyself" is urged, and immediately they submit themselves to a course of self-knowledge which leaves them confused and discouraged. They are not aware that confusion and discouragement are the surest signs of misdirection, so they go on digging deeper and deeper in the hope of finding the directive which will put them on the right way. "Know thyself" is an injunction which has to be approached with caution. Pressed too far it can do a lot of harm. As in responding to the call of voluntary poverty and penance there is a point at which one must lay off or one becomes encumbered with useless detail. "Know thyself if thou wouldst know God" has another side which reads "Get so interested in thyself that thou wilt leave no room for the knowledge of God." A better principle would be: know your nothingness, then turn away from it and go on to God.

It is true that St. Bernard claimed as objects of man's charity first God, second others, third self. But if it has to be in that order as regards charity, it has to be in that order as regards knowledge. The man who knows even a little about God and his neighbour should be able, by seeing himself in relation to God and neighbour, to see enough of himself to get along without too much specific study. He does not have to be constantly beating his breast and telling the world what a miserable sinner he is. He is not preoccupied by the need to oust a self which he knows in his heart can never be ousted. Instead he concentrates on something more constructive: he tries to introduce into his soul, by means of prayer and trust, as much of the power and love of God as will not only keep his preoccupation with himself under control but will prevent it from looming too large on his horizon of interest.

In spite of its concern with outward things, western society has never been so concerned about its inward troubles. Escape into materialism has shown itself to be a boomerang and we are all more locked up inside ourselves than ever: the boomerang has come back in the form of a ball and chain. That is why we bore one another so incessantly: we are fellows prisoners whose recreation is to talk about ourselves. We revel in our prison sentences while preaching freedom, we are so eager to outdo one another with our permissiveness that the only real freedom worth having is missed. Repetitive discussion about freedom to lead our own lives is followed by exhaustive examination to find out what our real lives are. This is not only because we live in a secular society which is not interested in the idea that the individual finds his fullest freedom and his true identity in the life of Christ; those of us who live in a professedly religious society are equally affected. We keep on redefining the nature and purpose of religion, recasting our expressions of worship so that they may fall in line with our ever changing psychological needs, purifying our concepts of virtue in the light of the current morality, exchanging new ideas of obedience for old, replacing one system of authority with another. The process is self-conscious, self-determining, self-valuing. When the spiritually minded person substitutes

"What do *I* feel about the problems I face" for "What does God feel about these things" he ceases to be a spiritual person.

Where religious education devotes too little attention to the avoidance of thinking about oneself, secular education devotes too little attention to the avoidance of talking about oneself. The two go together. A self-regarding spirituality reflects itself in self-denunciatory or self-congratulatory conversation – to the utmost weariness, as suggested above, of the listener. Where religious people tell one another how much they have to suffer, how generously they are offering themselves, how richly their sins have deserved punishment and so on, people who have little or no religion tell one another how successful they would be in their work or how happy they would be in their marriages if things were different, how they are not really to blame for their weaknesses, how much they have to put up with from the injustice of others, how all along the line they are being misunderstood. At the back of their minds, whether these people are religious or non-religious, lurks the haunting sense of guilt. They know that their excuses and rationalizations are sheer nonsense but do not know what to do about it. Among the first fallacies of today is the one which believes that worry and fear and guilt can be exorcized by talking about them. Do you wonder that we all become bores?

The advice to "air your grievances and you'll find they'll shrink to insignificance" is not always the salutary catharsis which people imagine it to be. Grievances have a way of expanding and multiplying. The idea that in order to rid yourself of an evil tendency all you have to do is take the lid off and let people have a look at it is not one which would recommend itself to those nearest to the gospel tradition. Spiritual authorities, almost down to our own time, have stressed the need to curb the passions and not let them out for a walk. The view was that if you give a potential vice half a chance it will break out into active expression and demand an increasing scale of satisfactions. Appetite for evil is a blackmailer, operating on a system of supply and demand. You do not lessen the pressure of temptation by yielding to it any more than you silence blackmail by giving in. The vices are here, inside us, only waiting for an excuse to get out into the open. The excuse is attractively presented by those who talk about the dangers of repression.

Without repression of some sort the whole concept of Christian morality falls to the ground. When he said that if your eye proved to be an occasion of sin you were to pluck it out, our Lord was preaching repression. If your hand becomes an obstacle to your salvation, our Lord told his disciples, you had better cut it off: repression again. When he said that lust and anger were to be smothered in the heart before they could break out into adultery and hatred, our Lord was preaching repression. When he called the rich young man to discipleship and perfection, when he told Peter and the apostles that those who would leave home and family and property for his sake could expect a reward, when he called for the same renunciations in the case of marriage to one wife, he was preaching repression. Not repression for the sake of repression but repression for the sake of a further good. The mistake which the critic of religion makes, particularly the modern critic who starts off with a built-in prejudice against frustration of any kind, is to see in religious

17

asceticism a calculated negation of a natural instinct and created good. The charge brought against the religious orders until quite recently has been that voluntary poverty, chastity, and obedience can do no possible good but on the contrary must restrict the development of the human personality. Today, admittedly, the tune is somewhat changing and the religious life is judged in terms of the welfare organization. Where the older tradition has been maintained, however, and where such things as silence, fasting, solitude and so on are observed, the same cry is raised about the evil of going against the natural appetites of man. Christian asceticism is not the conquering of human tendencies because they are evil but the conserving and containing of human tendencies with a view to man's true destiny. The principle is stated in the parable of the vine. "My Father is the vinedresser . . . every branch that bears fruit he prunes that it may bear more fruit."

The misleading feature for many in the question of whether to indulge or repress is that in the short term indulgence is judged to be more effective than repression. For example, people will say about themselves or others that it does them good to let off steam occasionally, and that it is better to fly into a rage than to smoulder and sulk. Possibly, but the momentary advantage has to be balanced against the long term disadvantage. From the way people talk you would suppose that by giving way to an irascible disposition you end up sweet-tempered, gentle and benign. Tensions may well be relieved by an outburst, but what is there to show that the tension is more harmful than the outburst? Those who make a case for anger are not slow to cite the anger of Christ when he threw the money changers from the temple. But surely the significant feature here is Christ's zeal for the sanctity of his Father's house. Our Lord did not fly into a rage which he could not control, was not releasing a tension which had become too much for him. He was directing a particular emotion towards a particular end, just as when he wept over Jerusalem or rejoiced over the successful mission of his disciples.

From the passion of anger, then, to the passion of sorrow. Sadness is in many ways a more important passion to get right than anger. This is partly because for most of us it is more habitual than anger — few people are in a constant state of fury whereas many are more or less sorrowful all the time — and partly because in the general opinion sorrow is less reprehensible than ill temper. Also it is less liable to make people look foolish. It is a passion nevertheless, and, unless checked, can be highly reprehensible. It can make people look foolish as well. Psychiatry, it must be supposed, would hardly advocate freedom of expression in the case of sadness. Even the most uninhibited would presumably deprecate indulgence of self-pity. Craving for sympathy, as everyone knows who has to listen to others, and who is faced with himself at his worst, is more addictive than any drug, more accumulative, more isolating. If only people could be persuaded to accept the incidence of suffering in their lives and then shut up about it, they would not only prevent their experience of it from being an almost total preoccupation but would have greater incentives for entering into the sufferings of others. Suffering, which ought to make us compassionate, may all too easily make us want to avoid the fellow sufferer. We are afraid of getting involved in the clinging of pity. Yet without pity we lose touch. "Having known misery" Dido is made to say to Aeneas,"I have learned to feel for the miserable." It is possible that wrapped too tightly in our shroud we may fail to learn this lesson.

If we leave our agonies to look after themselves instead of trying to prove their unique quality, we have more to give in the end. Nor can this diminish personal merit but on the contrary must add to it. It does not lessen our identification with Christ's passion to forget about our own. By making Christ's suffering the supreme objective — an objective more sanctifying than anything which could be effected in us by our own trials — we reduce the subjective element which inevitably alters focus and may even subordinate Christ's passion to our own.

Next take the passion of fear. Fear cannot but produce a defensive attitude in the mind. Worries, suspicions, false judgements. The orientation is inward-looking. Once again the result is a lack of concern for other people. Dread can make a man overlook the claims of justice and common morality. From here to the sealed off existence of the deliberately lonely is a short step. Having stepped, it is uncommonly difficult for the man who fears to step back. While craving for sympathy and understanding, people who fear and doubt reject society. They swing from a pathological desire to communicate their inmost beings to an equally pathological desire to avoid being commited. The danger of contracting out from society is that there is no longer a norm to refer to. There is a certain sanity attaching to the herd, and though the majority opinion may be ethically all wrong, and it may be the individual's duty to oppose it in every possible way, it is still true that the human race is designed as a body. To lose touch with the members of that body, to refuse to belong, is not only to lose touch with charity but to lose touch also with sanity. A man may, at the call of God's grace, transcend the sane and reasonable, but when he does it must be because of God's grace and not merely because his fear has turned him away from what is sane and reasonable. The way of grace is normally to act through sanity and reason; man goes against them at his peril.

For the person who has learned to take spirituality seriously the course is fairly clear. A deepening of the life of prayer may not cure an anxiety neurosis, the withdrawal syndrome, and other disorders, but at least it puts these things in better perspective. The spiritual life works upon the natural life, and never to greater advantage than when the natural life is developing idiosyncrasies. In all the hazards of life, interior and exterior, the programme is simply to "Cast all your care on God for he has care of you." "Once more I say unto you: trust . . . if the smallest things are outside your control, why worry about the rest . . . if God clothes the grass in the field, how much more will he look after you . . . set your hearts on his kingdom and all these other things will be given you as well." Since trust is at the root of our relationship with God it is astonishing that we apply it piecemeal, drawing upon it only when all else has failed or in matters of such universal interest as to make our personal contribution appear negligible.

Trust in the providence of God is not a heaven-sent formula for the indolent, not a way of bypassing responsibility with regard to social and material concerns. However much you commit yourself to God's care you still have to calculate, decide, work. Where fatalism and Christian trust part company is in the willingness to cooperate. You cannot simply say "it will take care of itself" and sit back. You do not have to worry about the outcome any more than does the fatalist but you do have to make the effort; you have to take on the affairs that come your way, knowing that they come from God and must be steered back again to him. Looked at in one way the outcome is in your hands, looked at in another the outcome is wholly in God's.

Moreover, there is this about trusting to the providence of God: when you most want to practice it you find yourself least confident in its efficacy. You may assent to the theory while doubting its application in your particular case. You say "I know God will provide" and then you add: "at least he would if I were in the right disposition for it, which I am almost certainly not." Whether you are trusting to the solution of an economic problem or to the question of your eternal salvation, these reflex thoughts keep coming in. You say "I believe God's mercy will cover all," and immediately you wonder if this is not a piece of superstitition, and if there is not possibly some catch in it. "Am I not putting my trust in a few magic syllables rather than in God? Is the term 'divine mercy' as valid as I am forcing myself to think it is, or is it just an open sesame which at the last moment will be found not to work?" Yes, in general of course the divine mercy must be what we are told it is, but does it really cover the insincere, the unfaithful, the hypocritical – *us*? Christ has atoned, Christ has redeemed, and then we remember that there are conditions . . . we must be in the right state of mind to receive the grace of redemption. What have we left out, what have we forgotten? Can it be enough just to wish our salvation, just vaguely to hope for it? It can only be trust that lifts us out of our panics and transforms the wishful fancy into a strong confidence.

There are texts in the gospels and epistles which develop the idea that all we have to do is to believe in Christ's name and we shall be saved. "Not by anything of your own" St. Paul tells the Ephesians, "but by a gift from God, not by anything you have done so that nobody can claim the credit." And to the Romans: "One man, Jesus Christ, will cause everyone to reign in life who receives the free gift, which he does not deserve, of being made righteous . . . however great the number of sins committed, grace was even greater . . . grace will reign to bring eternal life thanks to the righteousness which comes through Jesus Christ our Lord." At first reading the suggestion seems to be that almost without reference to man's cooperation, salvation is imposed on him from without whether he chooses it or not. But a closer look will show that Christ's universal salvific act assumes at least some desire on the part of man to be saved. There is nothing in scripture to show that God drags the obstinate atheist, still less the Christian who keeps up a state of blasphemy against the Holy Ghost, into heaven by the scruff of his neck.

The desire does not have to be couched in correct comprehensive, legal terms, the act of faith does not have to be logically worked out and signed. But desire and faith have to be there in some form or there is nothing for the consequences of desire and faith — namely salvation and sanctification — to operate from. There must be more in the profession of faith than the repetition of "Lord, Lord" if the kingdom of heaven is to be gained. Indeed the kingdom of heaven suffers violence and only the violent bear it away. Again our virtue must go deeper than that of the scribes and pharisees or we shall not get into the kingdom of heaven. "Unless you repent you will perish." Turning from our Lord's words to those of St. Paul, we see just as clearly that salvation is not automatic. "You know perfectly well that people who do wrong" he reminds the Corinthians, "will not inherit the kingdom of God: people of immoral lives, idolators, adulterers, catamites, sodomites, thieves, usurers, drunkards, slanderers and swindlers will never inherit the kingdom of God." When we read passages of this kind we echo the misgivings of the disciples when they heard from our Lord's lips how hard it was for a rich man to enter the kingdom of heaven. "Who can be saved then?" they asked. "For men" Jesus told them, "this is impossible; for God everything is possible." This must be the ground of our trust.

Some people are worriers by nature, and it is as worriers that they will have to find their way to God. To these, more than to any, the doctrine of rising above worry is of paramount importance. While the spiritual life has to be taken seriously, there is no merit in worry. For the earnest to imagine that their spiritual search should be accompanied by painful anxiety as to their present state and future chances is only to invite delusion. While nervous tension may be sent by God as a trial of faith and courage, it is not something to be courted as a sign of generous purpose. Nerves are a plague like any other, and more self-inspecting than most. The more objective the spirituality, God being the object sought rather than the perfecting of self, the better. Hair-splitting can be left to the theologians and legalists; simplicity is the aim in

Why?

the life of prayer. Our Lord speaks of the "single eye" which he wants his disciples to cultivate. Without it the singleness of purpose which is necessary to Christian service is harder than ever to achieve.

2

On Whose Authority?

On Jesus Christ's. "Anyone who wants to save his life will lose it, but anyone who loses his life for my sake will find it." These words come immediately after our Lord had said that anyone who aspired to being his follower must renounce himself and take up his cross. He was saying that the condition of discipleship is to let go of self-interest, is to forget about your own life in the effort to make his your pattern. This is what we have been considering in the foregoing chapter: trust in his merits and not in your own, attention to his teaching and not to reactions of your own. Again and again and over a wide range of issues, our Lord insists on the absolute necessity of trust. In the boat during the storm: "Why are you afraid? Have you no faith?" To the disciples who were disappointed at being unable to expel a devil: "Because of your lack of trust." When teaching them about prayer he instanced the case of a son instinctively trusting his father to provide what is best and not what is worst. Then there were the cures: "Go in peace; your faith has made you whole."

In this context one of the most telling passages is from St. Matthew's account of the sermon on the mount. Our Lord could not have spoken in clearer terms of the uselessness of anxiety, and, by implication, of the need to turn away from self-scrutiny. "I am telling you not to worry about your life: about what you are to eat, nor about your body and how you are to clothe it. Surely life means more than food and the body more than clothing. Look at the birds in the sky. They do not sow or reap or gather into barns; yet your heavenly Father feeds them. Are you not worth much more than they are? Can any of you, for all his worrying, add one single cubit to his span of life? And why worry about clothing? Think of the flowers growing in the fields; they never have to work or spin, yet I assure you that not even Solomon in all his regalia was robed like one of these. Now if that is how God clothes the grass in the field which is there today and thrown into the furnace tomorrow, will he not much more look after you, you men of little faith? So do not worry....."

A significant point in these gospel illustrations is that the members remain true to their species. If the birds were to try living like a fish, or if the grass behaved like a cloud, there would be no guarantee of divine protection. As human beings we can count upon the providence of God, but if we refuse to follow the laws which govern our human nature — acting either as angels or animals or devils — we break the contract and forfeit the claim. Man has to behave as a man, has to work and pray and love and suffer and use his freedom as a man. It is not the faintest use his acting as a machine or a vegetable. The flowers do not have to work and spin, because that is not their job, but if they refuse to draw nourishment from the soil and rain they die. Birds do not have to worry about where their next meal is coming from but they have to fly about and look for it, and if they sit on a branch all day waiting for it to come to them they starve. We must believe our Lord when he says that tomorrow will take care of itself, but the assurance rests on our trusting him today and working for him today.

From what he says about the necessity of denying ourselves in order to follow him, certain schools of spirituality have concluded that our Lord meant us to trample on the nature he gave us and to replace it with another. This is surely to miss the whole point. We do not get rid of self as though we were getting rid of an unsatisfactory servant; we go on employing self, the same natural self we were born with, but we allow God to purify the service and dictate its terms. In any case we cannot do much in the way of changing our nature, adding one cubit to our stature; what we can do is to live up to our nature at its highest level. By God's grace the self which was a slave becomes an adopted son. The family, not the species, is changed by this adoption. In this context trust amounts to believing in the work of grace, in the reality of God's action within the soul. And this is true whether we leave our material cares in his hands or look to him for guidance in the ways of the spirit. The more confidence we have in him the less time we shall waste in building up securities of our own.

In some respects it is easier to trust in the providence of God where material things are concerned than in matters of the spirit. The implication contained in the gospel passages quoted above is that the Christian must trust God as regards both. From turning over his prospects to God, the Christian should become less troubled about his progress. The overall result should be a deeper peace and sense of unity. It is not the peace of indifference, and the sense of unity is more than just a trick of the mind. In the long run indifference is the enemy of true peace, and the effort to acquire a mental knack is exactly the kind of thing which would bring on those self-regarding examinations and experiments which, as we have seen, are the bane of the spiritual life.

It is interesting to note that with the increasing popularity of yoga in the west a greater value is given to tranquillity and the relaxation of the mental faculties. Manuals are written about the close relationship between yogi and Christian mystics; practices of a contemplative kind are recommended; instructions relating to posture, time scale, diet and sleep are there for the asking. Christian yoga . . . and all you want is a mat. Suitably Christianized, these exercises may introduce countless souls to meditation who might otherwise never have come across it. The emphasis, moreover, on being relaxed in mind and body during the specific act of prayer cannot but be good. To many however (to me for one) there is more selfconsciousness in sitting with one's eyes shut, one's hands limp in the lap, one's muscles slack from the feet up, one's brain gently sloshing this way and that until a text or a holy thought comes ashore on the tide than there ever was in the bad old days when one was given points for meditation, compositions of place, conclusions and resolutions. In either case, the questions one asks oneself are much the same: Am I doing it right? What did the book say? Is it nearly over? Are other people as bad at this as I am; But in the case of the yoga techniques there can be the added fear — obviously not intended by the exponents and presumably not experienced by those who advance in the way approved

– that by cheating in the matter of posture or by looking round to see how one's fellow devotees are getting on, one might have to begin all over again. A false fear of course, but one which is not so likely to come up where traditionally Christian prayer is concerned. The Christian liturgy makes demands of the body, but these are routines which turn the mind out from itself and into the corporate act of worship. Indeed one of the advantages which liturgical prayer has over strictly interior and private prayer is that it tends to be more objective. Having put aside the highly methodical prayer of the nineteenth century meditation books we are now falling into the same sort of trap but at a less Christian level. New lamps for old, and in both cases the light shining on our own groping selves instead of upon the throne of God. No wonder we do not see the traps.

Still looking for evidence that Christ preferred the straight to the convoluted, we hear him telling his disciples that their almsgiving should be so uncomplicated in the criss-cross of motives that their left hands must not know what their right are doing. In the matter of fulfilling oaths to the Lord, he tells them, it is superstitious hairsplitting to distinguish between what is vowed in the name of heaven, in the name of Jerusalem, in the name of your head, in the name of the earth. None of this is necessary: it only gets you back to sorting out and qualifying and labelling your intentions. "All you need say is 'Yes' if you mean 'Yes', 'No' if you mean 'No'; anything more than this comes from the evil one."

The forthright approach, unreflexive and without explanation or apology, recommends itself to our Lord as we see in his treatment of Mary Magdalen, Zacchaeus, the Syrophoenician woman, the good thief. Nicodemus was a complex character but our Lord was extremely patient with him. Our Lord had no patience with the subtleties of the pharisees or with their shams, their legalism, their self-justification and false piety. In his parable about the pharisee and the publican our Lord shows clearly what kind of prayer he prefers. Prayer, far more than study or politics or creative art, is an index of a man's life, and where there is multiplicity in prayer there will be over-elaboration in the handling of life.

St. Antony of the Desert is recorded as saying "He does not pray perfectly who knows that he prays." This statement has often been taken to mean that in the higher reaches of prayer the human faculties are suspended in such a way as to render the person unconscious not only of what is going on all round him but even of the fact he is engaged in the act of prayer. It is possible, certainly, that St. Antony was alluding to a strictly mystical prayer, to the complete rapture or ecstasy in which God takes over the mind as well as the senses for the time being. But is it not much more likely, and more in keeping with the particular tradition which St. Antony represented, that the words refer to an unawareness, born of deliberate unconcern, as to the mere mechanics of prayer? It is at least arguable that St. Antony was in effect saying: When a man is praying perfectly he does not have to know that his intellect and will are at rest in God; he does not have to assure himself that his memory and imagination are putting no obstacles in the way of his prayer but rather helping it; he does not have to satisfy himself that he is carrying out the instructions in the book, and that he is making the required acts of praise, faith, hope, love, compunction, thanksgiving and petition. He is in God's presence, he wants to pray in any way God wants, and this is quite enough for him. The separate acts of prayer, and his own cerebral and emotional and chemical reactions, are taken for granted. He does not have to bother about anything except the fact that God is present to him. He does not have to bother much about that because in wanting to love him he is united to him.

In this connection it may be remembered that when St. Theresa of Lisieux was looking back over her life she told how it was her father's custom, when she was a quite small child, to take her out before she went to bed to show her the stars. He told her the names of the planets, how they were grouped and how far away there were believed to be, and how everything in the sky was the work of God's hands. Reflecting in later life on these occasions she judges that they marked for her the beginning of her prayer life. She was not conscious of setting her mind to pray, and there was no set form to her prayer, but in retrospect she thinks that the majesty of God so impressed itself on her little-girl mind as to evoke a response which must have been prayer. Awe and wonder. The greatness of God. No preoccupations with the worthlessness of self, no particular awareness that prayer is going on. Surely it was something of this kind which St. Antony had in mind when he made that remark about prayer.

Since this aspect of prayer is important, a further illustration will not be out of place. The scene is Lourdes and the time shortly before noon on a Sunday in August. A priest was standing with his back to the middle church, the crypt, and looking down from the parapet at the crowds which swarmed below him on the flat. Thousands of the faithful were coming away from the Mass which had just finished in the Pius X basilica, others were coming down the steps from the church immediately below him, the sick were being

wheeled to the Grotto, pilgrims were on their way to the
fountains, to the baths, to other Masses. Surveying such a
considerable gathering of souls, all with religious purpose in
mind, the priest felt that here was something he should be
able to write about, something which was good for a book or
at least an article. This in mind, he addressed himself to the
phenomenon of Lourdes. After about twenty minutes of this
he turned to the man who had been standing next to him
during all this time, a stranger who revealed himself later to
be a lecturer at a Canadian university, and gave to him the
product of his assembled thought. What the priest said was
this: "Faith is a wonderful thing." Not an observation of
startling originality. The Canadian professor turned his head
slowly, as though reluctant to take his eyes off the colour
and movement below, and said: "It surely is." That was all.
Two presumably educated men had nothing more to
contribute than the admission that the faith of Christians was
surely something wonderful. Thinking over the exchange
afterwards, back in his hotel, the priest felt something of a
fool. For all he knew the professor felt the same. It struck
him then that perhaps this was the kind of effect which
Lourdes was meant to produce. Awe, wonder, a sense of
stupidity and inadequacy. Lourdes seemed to show, as many
other aspects of the religious spectrum must show, that there
are some concepts too vast to be framed by the ordinary
arrangement of words, and that anything one says about
them is bound to sound silly. One might just as well stand
before them and say nothing. Better in fact to do this since
the effort to make phrases diverts from the main purpose.
Praise cannot be entirely wordless for long, but simply *being*
there in the state of praise is probably better than finding
terms in which to express one's praise.

If prayer, as suggested above, sets the pace for the rest of
life then it should follow that the simpler the person's prayer

the less fussy will be his work, suffering, relations with other people. In theory anyway this should be so, though as always the practice has to be thought out and deliberately made to conform with the theory. We find justification for this, once again, in our Lord's words. The general teaching is the same as that which we have been considering, namely "Do not let your hearts be troubled. Trust in God still, and trust in me." Taking first the question of work, it is clearly the will of the Father that we do not get through it anyhow: listlessly in mind and slipshod in execution. Our Lord gave us his example here. "As long as the day lasts" he said, "I must carry out the work of the one who sent me; the night will soon be here when no one can work." Over-anxiety about work is one of the evils of our time, what people will think of what we do. All this is unnecessary, and would not come up if we had more trust and approached things simply. "Do not worry beforehand what you are to say; no, say whatever is given you to say when the time comes; it is not you who will be speaking; it will be the Holy Spirit." We are so afraid of making fools of ourselves in what we mean to say that we retreat into nervous silence. This is only because we do not really believe that the Holy Spirit wants to guide us. We do not think the Holy Spirit is particularly interested in what we have to say. Considering we would not have anything to say if it were not for the Holy Spirit, whether in fact we get it said or not, this is to show a lack of appreciation for the Holy Spirit's activity in our lives.

In the same way it does no good to worry beforehand about what we may have to suffer. Our sufferings are in God's hands long before they are in ours. Are we sincerely convinced that God allows us to suffer only what we are capable of suffering? If we are not convinced of this it means that the problem of pain has not only got beyond us but has got beyond him. If God's providence means anything at all it must mean that he knows our condition and gives us the grace to turn our condition to his service and to our sanctification. We haunt ourselves with the thought that trials will come which we shall be unable to meet — with the thought that trials *have* come which we are unable to meet — and we forget that if this or that suffering were really too much for us God would so enlarge our capacity as to make the particular thing bearable. "What if I despair? What if I become a cause of scandal to others? What if I lose my reason? What if I die and those for whom I am responsible are left without anyone to provide for them?" God has allowed for all these contingencies; those questions would never be asked if we depended on God's providence and not upon our own resources. It is only because we imagine ourselves to be necessary to this or that humanly devised interlocking pattern that we fear the collapse of our hopes, of our health or mind, of our human relationships. If we thought about how necessary God's plans are to ourselves and others, we would worry less about suffering, temptation, frustration and despair.

Simplicity in our dealings with others is even less easy to acquire. But once again it should come with prayer and be proportionate to the simplicity of our prayer. Certainly it is inculcated in the gospel; one of the many charges our Lord levelled against the pharisees, scribes, and lawyers was lack of straightforwardness. Jerusalem's religious leaders were not as corrupt as they have been made out to be by later historians and commentators, but there is no doubt that they were bound hand and foot by legal, ecclesiastical, and liturgical red tape. The attention that we focus upon the trivial is so much attention withdrawn from the important. Our Lord's doctrine of love blew fresh air through the corridors of the temple, and the officials of the Establishment were shocked by it. It had never been put to them that the sabbath was made for man and not man for the sabbath, that the law of Moses was liberative not restrictive, that love of neighbour was meant to be universal and not selective. A revealing feature in the parable of the good Samaritan is that the hero of the story asked no questions. He performed his act of charity without a thought as to whether the injured man deserved being beaten up or not, without a thought about reward or reputation. The parable was a telling rebuke to those who connected charity with publicity. Recognition of virtue, according to the gospel, is a greater obstacle to virtue than the mockery of virtue. If a parade of almsgiving, penance, prayer has already received its reward, the prize given to those who suffer persecution for the sake of justice and for Christ's name may be withheld in this life but it mounts up in the next. Fanfare, diverting the intention, is to be avoided as yet one more complication in life. Hidden acts of charity, self-denial and worship, because God alone is witness, ensure simplicity.

All too often the exercise of Christian love (the term "Christian charity" has been weakened, denoting works of benefaction, so in the spirit of simplicity the word used here is frankly "love") is thrown into confusion by the emotions. Practically speaking, the problem of love is subjected to opposite pulls: excessive affection on the one side and excessive distaste on the other. Of the two, excessive distaste, being easier to see for what it is, causes less disturbance to one's peace of mind. Under the influence of sentiment, human relationships, which are meant to be reflections of the relationship between the soul and God, can become spirit-breaking, time-consuming, obsessive and mutually destructive. We can become so jealous, suspicious, appre-

hensive, conscience-ridden, motive-sorting, despairing, that
Christ's love is lost sight of, and the personal side of the
affair, even though it may be perfectly guiltless, comes to
occupy the whole horizon. Nothing so easily gives rise to
self-deception or so readily advances sanctification as love.
While of all subjects it is the one which must be considered
with a clear mind, it is at the same time the one about which
it is difficult to think clearly. There is nothing like emotional
stress for fooling a man as to his intentions, and unless he can
take a cool objective look at the issues involved, detaching
himself from the soft advice which he can get if he looks for
it, he will wake up one day to find his integrity has been
slipping. Only when the heart is not thumping can the still
small voice of God be heard.

It is difficult enough, heaven knows, to peel off the
romantic surface and concentrate on God-given love. But this
is where the spiritual life comes in to help. Prayer enables us
to move on from "the love of concupiscence" to "the love of
friendship" and thence to "the love of benevolence" and
pure charity. This is a more spontaneous process than it
sounds. The mistake here would be, on the showing of what
has been discussed in these pages, to tick off on one's fingers
each kind of affective actuation as it comes along. Thus we
do not have to say: "I must leave off feeling emotional about
this . . . I must start cultivating a more altruistic attitude . . .
how am I doing as regards pure charity? . . . anyway I am less
sentimental than I used to be . . . I think perhaps I may have
made it now." Much better to say: "I want God to get more
out of my affections than I get, and since he is love itself I
can safely leave the question of my love in his hands." This is
the simpler way, and it seems to work. We need only
remember the essential love, and leave it at that.

The recommendation to leave your depression alone, along with the other elements of life which are difficult to handle, can be left until later when it will receive separate treatment. The findings of this and the foregoing chapter can be summed up in the recommendation to trust and not to argue. St. Paul's attitude toward life inevitably follows: "I have learned in whatsoever state I am to be content therewith." Once you admit to being content you do not have to card-index your contentment, giving its causes, comparing it with previous experience, suspecting its validity, wondering how long it will last. Contentment is not quite like happiness, or even peace. Happiness and peace of mind are forever asking to be held up to the light to see if they are still there, but contentment can more easily be taken for granted. To be thanked for as coming from God, but not to be worried about. It will not leave us unless we let it.

God himself guarantees as much. In the *Benedictus*, the canticle of Zacharias, we read how "he remembers his holy covenant, the oath which he swore to our father Abraham, that he would grant us free from fear . . . to serve him in holiness and virtue, in his presence, all our days." A covenant is not a casual assurance that if all goes well perhaps something nice is in store; it is a pact sworn and sealed. In this case the guarantee is twofold, namely preservation from fear and the opportunity of lifelong service in virtue. Why, we ask ourselves at once, do we so seldom see the bargain, on man's side, fulfilled? It cannot be that God, by not giving us enough grace, fails to back his promises. It can only be because man hardly ever takes him at his word. The grace is there, but because man is trusting to other securities, the fear remains. God remembers, man forgets.

The mistake is to measure everything in terms of human calculation. Judged by the way we would behave, it is sheer madness to think of God not only as worthy to be trusted in every conceivable situation but as actually wanting to be trusted in every conceivable situation. If this fact were understood there would not be half the difficulties that there are about prayer, about coming to decisions, about meeting temptation. Fear would be reduced to a mere shrinking, a superficial natural reaction, and doubts in the same way would not be allowed to invade the deeper regions of the spirit. There may be times when we can get light upon a particular circumstance by judging what God would do if he possessed a finite mind like ours, but such occasions are not many. And in any case it is only guessing. It is true that our Lord brought home to his hearers the doctrine of the fatherhood of God by instancing a human father's concern for his son, but the doctrine of trust in general was preached not by comparison with human qualities but simply on the grounds of divine mercy and love. When talking about divine mercy and love it does not help a great deal to look into ourselves and raise what we see there to an unimaginable level. It helps much more to take what we know of divine mercy and love, and then to make the act of trust. This is not guesswork but good sense.

Our estimate of how the divine mind operates is bound to be wrong on almost every count, but we cannot go wrong in relying on his love and mercy. St. Basil in his sweeping ways says that for man to form concepts of God is to be guilty of blasphemy, and if this statement shocked his contemporaries it should not shock us who have witnessed man's arrogance in proposing altogether new ideas as to the nature and function of God. St. Basil was all in favour of man stretching out to God in contemplation but he would not have at all approved of the modern trend which subjects God to psychological analysis.

For the finite mind to surrender in absolute trust to a mind which is infinite must involve, humanly speaking, risk. It is a risk for two reasons: first because as has just been pointed out the finite mind knows so little about the workings of the infinite mind, and secondly because an absolute authority can do what he likes with his subjects. God made us; we belong to him. But if we are talking about risk there is far more risk in rebelling against him than in surrendering to him. Experience shows that those who take the risk of giving in to God at every point of their lives — the saints are wise enough to do this — no longer think of risk. The people who are haunted by it are those who do not take it. To refer once again to the gospel it is a question of choosing between two masters. You cannot comfortably serve mammon because when you try to you feel you are in the wrong box. You may not much want to serve God, but when you try to you know you are in the right place.

3

Children as Models

That our Lord should urge his disciples to follow the example of children was considered important enough to be recorded by three of the four evangelists. In almost identical words, Matthew, Mark, and Luke tell how when children came to him, he rebuked those grown ups who wanted to turn them away. St. Mark quotes our Lord as saying "I tell you solemnly, anyone who does not welcome the kingdom of God like a little child will not enter it" and adds that he gave the children his blessing. St. Luke repeats the reprimand but does not mention the blessing. All three say that our Lord made the point that the kingdom of God properly belongs to children. There is much to be learned from these references, and an enormous amount has been written and preached as to their import. But even if what follows has an over-familiar ring it can be seen at once how relevant the texts are to the argument under review.

Our Lord's words are clear, but the psychological difficulty remains. How do I approach the kingdom of God as a child when I am not a child? Nicodemus finds the same difficulty when he is told by our Lord he must be born again. However vividly I remember my childhood, however apparent the fact that my adult attitudes have been largely shaped by what I learned as a child, however genuine my affection for the very young, I know very well that the authentic quality has gone for good. Sometimes in a dream I get the feel of it again, and there are sudden unexpected associations which pull me back across the years, but then I wake up or the magic moment passes and I am back on the wrong side of the barrier. So our Lord cannot be referring to that kind of experience or we would have no assurance of entering the kingdom at all. Surely he is not saying we must recapture the sense of it in order to express its characteristic virtues; he is saying we must cultivate those virtues which in a child do not have to be cultivated because they are there already.

The aim for us who are grown up will be twofold. On the negative side it assumes the avoidance of tendencies not normally associated with small children: suspicion of others, double dealing, taking malicious advantage, giving scandal and rejoicing in scandals, resentment against God's will, gloating over the failures of others, pride, self-pity, despair. Infants who showed such inclinations would be monsters. On the positive side it tries to develop habits, instinctive in children, of trust, undiscriminating love, acceptance of life as it presents itself from day to day, taking happiness for granted and not questioning it, looking out for the good which is enjoyed with unselfconscious pleasure.

In putting children before us as our models our Lord does not expect us to imagine ourselves back in the state of innocence which was ours before we reached the age of reason. This would be mental hypnosis. It is not innocence so much as integrity that has to be aimed at. The way in which mature beings can benefit by our Lord's injunction is to work at simplicity and dependence. This is a viable programme. If we cannot attain to the simplicity of babies or saints – much less of God – we can at least free ourselves from the complexity of secular, rationalistic, hedonistic thought. Nor does the mind, in the cause of simplicity, have to turn into a vegetable. It remains a mind, and in fact operates at its highest capacity because uncluttered by concerns which would otherwise dissipate its energy. The history of sanctity is full of examples of how souls who started off as highly complicated individuals, some of them so introverted and sensititve as to be almost neurotic, became, under the influence of grace and by judicious direction, more simple, direct, and objective than would have been thought possible by those who knew them earlier. In the same way souls of limited intelligence and practically no education acquire, in some cases quite without their knowledge, a singular wisdom. The classic example of an extremely subtle mind, though not one of exceptional academic training, is that of St. Theresa of Lisieux. Self-examining and ready to burst into tears at the slightest snub, imagined or intended, this complicated young woman might well have gone from breakdown to breakdown had she not gone to Carmel, and, once there, had she not taken herself in hand. What emerged from all this was the famous "way of spiritual childhood." Advance toward spiritual childhood went step by step with increasing simplicity, whether in the sphere of prayer or in the deliberately schooled attitude towards outward things: the self in subjection to the will, the will in subjection to God: spiritual childhood.

There is also, as already suggested, the question of dependence. It never crosses the child's mind *not* to depend upon others. In the early stages it can do nothing for itself; all along the line it relies upon help which it neither questions nor claims as a right nor is grateful for. The help always seems to be there and the child uses it. As the years roll on, and the help is gradually withdrawn, the child has to manage more and more on its own. But it still leans wherever it can, knowing that its parents are there to be leaned on. Only when the child has grown to maturity, no longer qualifying as a child, does this dependence change direction. So when our Lord is telling mature people to become as little children he is demanding the quality of dependence as much as that of simplicity. The difference now is that people must depend knowingly and with gratitude upon the providence of God. Knowingly but not analytically, and as far as possible without hesitation or reflex thought. Always, however real the dependence on God, there will have to be a dependence on creatures, too. Where the supernatural is relied upon to the total exclusion of the natural there would be the danger of presumption, or at least of superstition. If it was one of our Lord's temptations on the mountain to defy the laws of nature by jumping from the pinnacle of the temple, it can well be a temptation to us to make no provisions in the natural order and to presume upon God's miraculous intervention. The right balance has to be kept here. We take the ordinary means at our disposal and then leave the outcome to the wisdom and power of God. It is not only the end proposed that is his will; the means which lie to hand are equally his will. It is paying no compliment to God to throw away the means in the name of achieving, by the way of pure faith, the required end. If we were wholly spiritual beings, like the angels, we would not be tied down as we are to the support provided by the material world. But God, in defining our nature, has given us earthly things to think about as well as heavenly. Where we must be careful is in the direction of our choosing. It must be our will to depend more upon God's providence than upon our own circumspection or temporal opportunity.

Another attribute of the child which is worth considering is freedom from social convention, snobbery, and cant. Children are often envied for the wrong things and pitied for the wrong things. From one point of view the infant is seen as fortunate in having no responsibilities or worries, not a care in the world; again it is seen as unfortunate in being a prison to its crib, its baby carriage, its time for going to sleep and the miserable kind of food it is expected to eat. Whichever way you look at it, the child possesses the immense advantage over the rest of us in not being cramped by the shibboleths of society. The infant is free of those rules and customs, arbitrary for the most part but hideously binding, which engender fear, embarrassment, shame, and every sort of self-examination in the adult. The baby is not afraid of making a fool of itself, of wearing the wrong clothes, of speaking with a bad accent, or dropping into an idiom which is unacceptable, of not having read the right books or known the right people or in general learning the rituals which happen to be fashionable at the moment. The baby is not blamed for being ignorant of these things, for being out of the class war and the contemporary swing. The adult is, unfairly, so blamed. But the man who is truly single minded and simple rises above blame, embarrassment, self-appraisal, dread.

As in the case of even the soundest endeavours there can be exaggeration here. And self-deception. In the belief that he is showing a childlike directness and simplicity a man may be boorish, inconsiderate, stubborn. Not all the child's characteristics are enviable, and some, in a grown up person, would be reprehensible. The man who kicks his car because he cannot find the key is not being childlike but showing childish ill-temper. The man who sulks and refuses to eat because the oysters he ordered are not to be had is not being childlike but immature. The woman who insists on watching television when everyone else wants to talk or who plays a game in her own way to everyone else's discomfort is not imitating her little daughter's candid nature but is being downright selfish. So it looks as though even now we still have to make distinctions and reservations in our search for simplicity. But this does not take away from the principle that we serve both God and man better when there is nothing up our sleeve but the niceties of our definitions. There is a lot to be said for the line which goes the shortest way between two points.

Then there is the ever articulate question of sex. For this we refer to the story of the fall of man. The uglier and unreconciled implications of sex were revealed only after the disobedience had been committed: then it was that they saw they had no clothes on and felt ashamed. Selfconsciousness had come to them, and things were never to be the same again — for anyone. Simplicity which would have been effortless would henceforth be something to strive after, and love which would have been safe would henceforth have to be safeguarded. There could still be peaceful submission but it would have to come as the result of conflict. There had been no fear before, but now that they had been caught out, our first parents knew what it was like to dread the justice and just punishments of God. There had been no loneliness before but now that they had turned down the friendship of God, Adam and Eve were alone with one another, and this was no substitute for the companionship of God.

We get an idea of true psychological simplicity when we consider how Adam and Eve's centre of interest before the fall was God. All their faculties were trained on and at rest in him. This did not involve strain any more than their prayer involved strain. For them it was natural to want God at the centre of their lives and to want to give him glory. It was only when their centre of focus, as the result of the duality caused by sin, became themselves that opposing tensions made themselves felt. It is these tensions which fallen humanity still has to wrestle with, still has to draw into unity. Full harmony is impossible – the chaos resulting from the fall has seen to that – but at least there can be some sort of order in men's lives. At least they can aim at simplicity. In a world without God, and even in a world which professes belief in God but does not much back up that belief, there are so many centres of attraction apart from God that the idea of trying to unify and simplify hardly enters people's heads. They are so conscious of many appetites within themselves, all clamouring for satisfaction, that the urge is rather to diversify, to express themselves in as many directions as possible. A materialistic world ministers only too efficiently to the scattering of interests. So with distraction and dissipation to compete against, simplicity, either inward or outward, is not easy to come by.

Turning from man's fall to his redemption we move from Adam's original and unconscious simplicity to the chosen and conscious simplicity of Christ. Here it must be remembered that Christ, though conceived without original sin, took on sin. In becoming truly man he assumed the liabilities of man. He "bore the weight of our sin": the whole consequence of the fall. He suffered accordingly every temptation known to man. This is important in the present context because it might be thought that Christ, untouched by sin, would enjoy the prerogatives of Adam before the fall as well as the natural simplicity of innocent children. But the point of the incarnation was to share, without himself falling, man's *fallen* condition and to atone for the sin of disobedience. For Christ to have become the kind of person Adam was when he was innocent would have been to stop short of the essential crisis. Again to have maintained the simplicity of childhood would have been little use as an example to us who are not children. Infants are not troubled by vices which will trouble them later on. Christ in his infancy was not troubled by them either. But because he grew from real infancy into real boyhood, and from real boyhood into real manhood, he suffered the temptation to real vices. In our own temptations we can expect from him an understanding born of actual human experience.

Applying the above to our subject of simplicity we see in Christ the deliberate cultivation of an attribute reflected from the Father and lost with the fall. Though man's lost status is redeemed in one act of atonement his fragmented psychology has still to be mended bit by bit. Simplicity is something which we have to learn directly from Christ, and less directly, from the example of his saints. We should be able to learn it from reason and experience, but very few of us do.

Though inward simplicity is more important than outward, it is difficult to see how the inward can flourish unless a serious effort is made to simplify one's outward life. There are already so many contradictions and inconsistencies in man that it only adds one more if he claims to be inwardly integrated and serene while he cheerfully entangles himself in every sort of mess. A man may be unmethodical by nature but this is no reason why he should choose to live in a bear-garden.

Look at the simplicity of the settings Jesus choose: Bethlehem's manger, Nazareth's workshop, the small towns and villages of Galilee where he preached. The simplicity of those closest to him: Mary and Joseph, his cousin John, the shepherds who came to adore, the apostles, the household at Bethany. The simplicity of living for thirty years among people who had not noticed his existence until he started preaching and working miracles. The unobtrusive exterior pointing to and expressing the inward attitude.

We know very little about the daily life at Nazareth but we would not dream of connecting it with restlessness, bustle, fidgets and fuss. In our kind of society it is becoming increasingly difficult to cut down on non-essentials. It is difficult enough to distinguish between what is necessary and what is not. In primitive societies the problem does not come up because people have to subsist on what they can find: what is there is necessary, and what is not there is not known about. But with us there are so many things to be had that we come to think more and more of them are vital to our existence. The accumulation syndrome. Solomon was a victim of this, but then by his time Hebrew civilization was far from primitive.

A more simple order of living, and the classic model for us, is primitive Christianity. We read how the early church turned its back on the materialism of the age. "The whole group of believers was united, heart and soul; no one claimed for his own use anything that he had, as everything owned was held in common . . . none of their members was ever in want, as all those who owned land or houses would sell them and bring the money from them to present it to the apostles; it was then distributed to any members who might be in need." If we cannot return to that standard we can certainly prevent ourselves from getting any farther away from it than we are already. Western civilization is becoming so computerized, automationed, air-conditioned, thermostated, washing-machined, electric-cookered, and otherwise controlled that instead of simplicity coming to us in the ordinary course we have to go out of our way to find it. We need to form an early Christian conscience on these matters and not assume that contemporary standards are necessarily ours by God's kind permission. Luxury alters our judgement, practical as well as spiritual, so that we go after the things that are not of God and give excellent reasons for doing so. Luxury corrupts, and absolute luxury corrupts absolutely. The sensualist (the rationalist, too, and probably the biologist) says "Love your life and you shall find it." Christ says "Love your life and you shall lose it." The world and Christ have different conceptions of life, and of what ministers to the fulfilment of life, so those who profess to follow Christ must face the challenge of detachment with a clear eye.

We do not have to envy little children their continence or their abstaining from alcohol but we may well envy them in their relatively few possessions. Travelling first or second class is a matter of indifference to them. They do not ask for expensive meals, and so long as they do not see other people eating something which they prefer they will eat pretty well anything. Children are far more adaptable than the rest of us to houses and furniture and surroundings generally. No wonder he who said that while birds had their nests and foxes had their lairs, "the Son of Man had nowhere to lay his head" gave us children to imitate. Aptly does St. Paul warn the Corinthians against allowing their "ideas to get corrupted and turned away from the simplicity that is in Christ."

A child's dishonesty is not difficult to detect. Its natural candour makes it difficult for a child to hang on to a lie for any length of time. But when a child has grown older, and has got used to the idea of duplicity, the mind is not as transparent as it was. Deceit can become an interest, a skill. Christ forgives this kind of child as readily as he forgives its elders, but he would not speak of it in the same terms as those used about the children who were "not to be despised for that their angels in heaven are continually in the presence of my Father who is in heaven." Some of our Lord's strongest denunciations are reserved for those who give scandal to the young and cause them to lose their innocence and simplicity. After saying that anyone who receives a little child in his name welcomes him, he goes on to say that "anyone who is an obstacle to bring down one of these little ones who have faith in me would be better drowned in the sea with a great millstone round his neck." Our Lord makes allowance for the loss of childlike qualities because it is in the nature of growing up that change is valued, that lessons are learned from experience, that new incitements are felt. "Obstacles indeed there must be" he says, "but alas for the man who provides them."

Nobody could have been more straightforward than St. Paul. He tells the Corinthians: "There is one thing we are proud of, and our conscience tells us it is true: that we have always treated everybody, and especially you, with simplicity and sincerity which come from God, and by the grace of God we have done this without ulterior motives. There are no hidden meanings in our letters apart from what you can read for yourselves." St. Paul, himself an intellectual, is very much aware of the dangers of intellectualism. To the same Corinthians, who regarded themselves as a sophisticated lot, he wrote: "Where are any of our thinkers today? Do you not see how God has shown up the foolishness of human wisdom? If it was God's wisdom that human wisdom should not know God it was because God wanted to save those who have faith through the foolishness of the message that we preach ... God's foolishness is wiser than human wisdom, and God's weakness is stronger than human strength ... it was to shame the wise that God chose what is foolish by human reckoning ... those whom the world thinks common and contemptible are the ones that God has chosen — those who are nothing at all to show up those who are everything. The human race has nothing to boast about to God." We are all children and the less we boast of our knowledge the safer we are. We have no knowledge but what is lent to us by God. All wisdom is his wisdom.

"God has made you members of Christ Jesus and by God's doing he has become our wisdom, and our virtue, and our holiness, and our freedom." By acknowledging the truth of this, and by working it into our everyday consciousness so that it becomes the ground of all our thought and action we get as near as it is possible to get to true spiritual childhood.

4

The Divine Simplicity

Theologians tell us (St. Basil notwithstanding) that God is infinitely simple. This means apparently that all his perfections come together into unity. God is a single being, every divine attribute blending into one; we are fragmented beings, compounded of many different tendencies, at variance with ourselves — with a hundred selves at once. A Jesuit theologian, Father Nieremberg, says that in God the diverse qualities of infinite perfection form one absolute identity amounting to a single entity. "There is no distinction between his power and his wisdom, between his wisdom and his justice, between his justice and his goodness, his goodness and his providence, his providence and his infinity. We see every excellence united in the simplicity of his nature."* Somehow we have to reflect this in our own lives and in our own natures. At the human level obstacles abound, but the grace of simplicity, relative to our degree, is present in every life.

* La Beaute de Dieu, p.61

If God is the sum of all perfection, and if we on our natural finite plane are called to grow in likeness to him, an affinity of some sort must be possible. "Be you perfect as your heavenly Father is perfect" is not so fantastic a summons, an order even, as at first sight it looks. What it means is: "Just as the Father is perfect in his way, which is an infinite and absolute way, so you must be perfect in your way which is finite and relative." We are made in his image and likeness, and if there is no means of achieving this likeness then the terms of man's creation stand for nothing.

Consequently this idea of God's simplicity being imitable is no mere fancy, is not an oratorical flourish which we can regard as mere embroidery. It is a practical reality which must be worked upon and put into active exercise. It is evidently possible for man to arrive by grace at what God is by nature. Not fully, or man would be equal to God, but more than figuratively. Though man may be handicapped from the start, he possesses one great advantage in his search for unity: he knows that God, having created human nature, knows the limitations of that nature. God has watched man fall and has picked him up; he knows the weakness of man and that there will be more falls to come. But this is the way he has made us human beings, and though the situation may not be ideal it is at least redeemable. That is what the incarnation and redemption are about: in Christ we fallen creatures are re-deemed worthy to stand before the Father and reflect him.

It is an astonishing fact, but nevertheless true, that God likes us as we are. Not only in the mass but individually. Yet in spite of the parable of the prodigal son we still make the mistake of qualifying the doctrine of divine fatherhood. We do not see how God's love can really be all that it is made out to be, how it can bear comparison with a human father's tolerance for a human son's defects. We may not always argue, as suggested above, from human experience when estimating divine operations, but where love is concerned we have only love to go upon, and the projection from personal to doctrinal knowledge has evangelical authority. In the case of simplicity it works the other way: we look at the oneness of God and try, from what we know of it, to integrate ourselves.

One of the main obstacles to personal integration, whether you look upon it as spiritual maturity or spiritual childhood, is nervous apprehension. In the parable of the sower it is the *cares* as much as the riches of this world which can be the cause of halted growth. Worry and insecurity are the bane of modern man's existence. We hesitate, dither, fear, until trust is reduced to a trembling wishfulness. Confidence in God may have to be tested by doubt, indeed must be, but doubt is not meant to bring about a mental paralysis. Countless examples could be drawn from the lives of the saints to show how a shaky hope is stiffened by the practice of prayer into firm belief. St. Francis of Sales, who could not have been more serene in later life and whose calmness soothed the fears of others, was fully persuaded when studying Calvinist writings as a young man that he was destined for hell. St. Benedict Joseph Labre was at first haunted by the thought of hell, but by the end was wholly possessed by the thought of heaven. Even the efficient St. Teresa of Avila had to overcome dreads which were purely imaginary. The sensible, simple, normal St. Margaret Mary was terrified at the beginning of her spiritual life that in the convent she might be forced to eat cheese. All nerves. All lack of integration. All interior disunity where there should have been unification on the model of divine unity. God has no nerves but if he understands us whom he has made the way we are he must be able to compassionate the nervous.

But we must be careful here or yet another obstacle to simplicity will declare itself. Weakness can be condoned on the grounds of being highly strung. Job was highly strung, but he is described as simple and just. His simplicity lay not in his nervous system but in his resignation. Jacob as a boy was probably extremely high strung — he was certainly extremely devious — but he ended up a balanced and maturely spiritual character. Elias, delighting in dramatic effect, was as temperamental and sensitive as any modern performer on the stage, but consider what he learned on Mount Horeb after his triumph over the priests of Baal. The lesson is for us as much as it was for him: God was not in the hurricane, was not in the earthquake, was not in the fire, but was in the gentle breathing of the breeze. Elias was told moreover to go back the way he had come and start again. His way was to Damascus and to spiritual childhood, to the way of simplicity which is the way of the presence of God.

From trying to stretch out to the simplicity of God in prayer we become not only more objective but more true. Away from the selfishness which creates fog and confusion, we become, at least in the estimation of others, more transparent. When we stop making estimates of our own progress we become more open, more artless, less concerned about how others are thinking of us. All that matters to us is the life of God to which we have become heirs. We have dispossessed ourselves and become Christ's adopted sons. We can say with St. Paul: "I live now not I but Christ lives in me. I pray now not I but Christ prays in me and through me." How can this *not* lead to simplicity? God breathes himself into us and we breathe back. He breathes his life, his prayer, his virtue into us, and we breathe back. No merit of ours. "As by the Lord's spirit" says St. Paul, "we are transformed into the same image from glory to glory." Lacking virtue of our own, we borrow from his. It is our infirmity which invites the infusion of his strength.

When the author of the Canticle says "you know yourself not, my beautiful one" he was saying what St. Thomas was to say, speaking of the soul's relationship with Christ: "The bride did not know where to look." "You were within me" says St. Augustine to our Lord, "and I was without." Perhaps it is only the saints who understand the implications of this doctrine. They are the ones who write about it most, encouraging the rest of us to look more deeply into its mystery. St. John Damascene speaks of God as the "infinite ocean of being" and how we, who are not even a drop, can, by his grace, take in that whole ocean. Quoting words of our Lord addressed to her soul, St. Catherine teaches the same truth: "I am he who is: you are she who is not." The answer must surely be that we appreciate the implications only to the degree that we are detached from material things. When the drop of water is no longer preoccupied with living its temporal life, is no longer full of itself, it is made capable of taking in the infinite life of grace. We become shut in upon ourselves either by the senses or by the cares and fears of life, and because we want to live more fully we in fact restrict our capacity for living. It is a curious paradox that the man who wants to look at God alone is the one who ends up seeing all that is to be seen. "What could they not see" asks St. Gregory, "who see him who sees all?"

It is alarming to reflect that matter can blind us to the one supremely important fact of our lives, namely that we are made in the image and likeness of God. Once we lose interest in this piece of knowledge, neglecting to develop that image and likeness, we begin to lose interest in being what we are essentially designed to be. Consequently we become more and more likely to develop a false image and likeness. Instead of seeing ourselves reflected in God and God reflected in us, we see only ourselves as the entity worth looking at and there is no room for looking at God. St. Paul exhorts the Corinthians to focus their vision on the invisible and not the visible "for visible things last only for a time, and the invisible things are eternal." He further argues that the visible is designed to be the means by which the human mind may reason its way to the acknowledgement of the existence of the invisible. If a man becomes transparently honest and selfless in the measure that he directs his effort towards the unity of God, it is also true that to such souls the things of life become increasingly transparent — as when a strip of film is held up to the light so that what has been photographed can be seen before it is projected on the screen. Nature and art and human affairs, instead of appearing as ends in themselves and therefore as constituting obstacles to the vision of God are now in focus. God is seen through the film; the colour and design and sequence and character of what has been photographed make sense at last. So it is by the same paradox that the man who takes on faith the film's colour production, composition and so on views the whole story from the credits to the curtain, while the man who looks only for entertainment has to satisfy himself with the stills.

Considered now from God's point of view, the fact that the creature can reflect the creator means that God derives glory from seeing himself in the whole widescreen range of the created transparency. He sees through the material and temporal film to his own image of which the film is but a reproduction. So not only are people, nature, art, finite existence, temporal affairs scaled with his mark but, more intimately, they are his self-portrait. They do not merely carry his authentic signature in the corner of the canvas but bear the authentic image and likeness which he alone can impart. "We are God's work of art" St. Paul writes to the Ephesians, "created in Christ Jesus to live the good life as from the beginning he had meant us to live it." Where there is a masterpiece there is more of the master than can be found anywhere outside the master himself. So to the same Ephesians St. Paul can write: "You, too, have been stamped with the seal of the Holy Spirit to make his glory praised." As an indication of the simplicity which is here assumed we read in the same chapter that God "would bring everything together under Christ as head, everything in the heavens and everything on earth, and it is in him that we are claimed as God's own . . . chosen to be for his greater glory."

In the human order we know how misleading self-portraits can be. Compared with a photograph or with the artist himself, the painting can often be found to show very little likeness. It is the same, unfortunately, when God looks for his own likeness in us and sees only a halfhearted copy, a blurred caricature. He has remained the unchanging model, has provided all the material, has even done the work himself. Then we have come along and botched the masterpiece. Where he should have been able to step from the frame in person (as in *Rudigore*), we, either feeble imitators or fraudulent forgers, stand exposed for what we are. Instead of "I live not I, but Christ lives in me" it is "I live very much myself, and Christ lives outside me." And so all along the line when it could have been "I pray now not I, I work now not I, I resist temptation now not I, I practice virtue now not I, but Christ does all these things in me and for me and through me."

Change the metaphor and you have a man looking down a well and saying something into it. The clarity with which he sees his face and hears his voice will depend upon how deep the well and how close to the surface the water. Even at best he is not getting his essential self out of the well, but he is getting something which nobody but himself could get out of it. When God looks down the well of his creation he is not getting his essential self out of it – though the Pantheists would have held that his reflection is himself – but he is getting what nobody else could either put there or take out. For us, the reflections of his face and echoes of his voice, the main concern should be to keep the surface of the water unruffled by multiplicity and at the right level.

It is not hard, then, to see why, as given in the Book of Proverbs, "God's communication is to men of simple heart." Like calls to like, and communicates itself to like. In order to answer this call and receive what is ours for the asking we have only to unlearn worldly wisdom and prepare ourselves for the communication of grace from grace itself. We do not have to be mystics or intellectuals to condition our minds to infused light. All we need is singleness of purpose. "If your eye be single, your whole body will be full of light" St. Matthew records our Lord as saying. One who was both a mystic and an intellectual but who was at the same time simple enough to be graced with great light, John Ruysbroeck, wrote as follows: "By what way must we go if we are to appear before God? By the way of likeness to God ... simplicity of intention gathers into unity the scattered forces of soul and unites the spirit with God. Moving through and penetrating all places, all created things, simplicity finds God in his deep mystery ... wherever possible we must cultivate simplicity above all things: full of faith in God it includes hope and charity ... it is simplicity that will gain for us the inheritance prepared from all eternity."

One of the interesting points about the above quotation is the way in which the author seems to identify simplicity with the three major virtues. Ruysbroeck says that simplicity must be cultivated "above all things." Surely he is forgetting, we say at once, that the virtue to be cultivated *above all things* is charity. But of course he is not forgetting charity at all, as his next sentence shows, but assuming it. Simplicity without charity would not "gain for us our eternal inheritance" any more than would "the gift of prophecy . . . faith sufficient to move mountains" or voluntary poverty or martyrdom by burning.

What he is telling us to do is to practice faith, hope and charity *in* simplicity, and that by aiming at simplicity for the love of God we find ourselves increasingly faithful, hopeful, charitable. The same idea is contained in our Lord's words to Martha, the busy sister of the contemplative Mary: "You are concerned about many things but *one* thing is necessary." Once we have love as our whole objective, as Mary had, then we practice it, together with faith and hope, in simplicity.

From this it may be seen how the charity which is practiced by human beings reflects the charity which is found in God. God *is* charity, so whatever love there is in us is God's — is God himself unified, is both the cause and effect of man's unified charity. Man's charity may express itself now in public worship, now in private prayer, now in apostolic work for souls and now in the love of husband or wife, but while there are diversities of activity there is unity at the source. In this activist age the tendency is to diversify when the aim should be to bring about a synthesis, a unification. If from the visible things of God's creation we can come to know the invisible God himself, who is one, then from the lovable things of God's creation we should be able to appreciate the unity of God's love from which all lovable things derive their value.

As God imparts love, so man must impart love. The more perfectly man loves God the more simply he imparts God's love to others. "Contemplation" says Thomas Aquinas, "diffuses itself," cannot remain locked up inside the mind. In Martha love diffused itself in one way, in Mary another. The source and substance were the same in each sister, the manner was different. The love coming from each found its destination, but the less agitated love was pronounced the better because it more closely resembled the love which God has for us. It more closely resembled also the love which exists between the Persons of the Blessed Trinity. Even this absolute love which exists between the Father, Son, and Holy Spirit, which you would think could not possibly need to impart itself did in fact impart itself in the act of creation. And has imparted itself ever since. It is the reason of existence, and if for one moment it were to confine itself to the mutual love of the three Persons – which love could do without loss to itself – creation would cease to be.

Whatever it was before the coming of Christ, the religious obligation after Christ's coming could not be more clear. "Other foundation no man can lay but that which is laid which is Christ Jesus." St. Paul comes back to this concept of Christ supporting the whole structure not only of the church but of humanity in general and in particular of the individual soul. Christ the corner stone, Christ the head of the body, Christ whose spirit works through every gift, Christ whose resurrection is the ground of all our faith and the surety of all our hope. Without the dominant theme of Christ running through the whole of our service and spirituality, our faith is vain. At every point, from our baptism in him to our final resurrection in him as our guarantor, as the sole certain promise, as the substance and foundation on which our destiny rests. This in itself bears out the principle of unification and simplicity.

Anyone who looks up the word "simple" in a concordance will be struck by the number of times it appears in both the Old and the New Testaments. The opening verse of the Book of Wisdom tells us to "seek God in simplicity of heart" and we find the same sort of exhortation, differently worded, throughout the wisdom literature of the Old Testament. Mostly the writer warns against what he calls a "double heart" or "lying lips" or "devious speech", but the idea is the same. The New Testament echoes this in its more positive sense, St. Paul urging the Romans to obey with a "simple heart," the Ephesians to fear God "in simplicity of heart," the Corinthians to give to the poor with a "simple heart" and to "exercise authority in a spirit of simplicity." St. James's advice is, again, to avoid the hypocrisy and hairsplitting of the world. It would seem that in apostolic times circumlocution and equivocation were common currency just as much as they are in ours. Perhaps this is why the example set by the early Christians as mentioned in the Acts was in such marked contrast to the prevailing standard. Nothing reproaches us more than forthrightness in the conduct of those whose ideals we are supposed to share but to which we have given only a notional assent.

To sum up, then, the spiritual life directs us to aspire, in our human degree, to the unity which is increasingly seen to be in God. St. Peter says that we become by grace what God is by nature: partakers of the divine nature. By the Word made flesh the Father expresses himself in the Person of Christ without loss to the unity of the divine nature. Without loss to the unity of the divine nature the Holy Spirit is expressed in the human soul and in the created order. In case it might be thought from what has been said earlier that God decided one day to extend the scope of divine love to another order of being, namely the created order and in particular to human beings, we can remind ourselves that every outward thing, material and natural and spiritual, has existed from all eternity in the mind of God. Man is not a sudden happy inspiration who turned out to be not so happy after all. It was only man's physical existence which came into being with time. Our souls were there, in the mind of God, before our bodies found a place in the created order. By the incarnation the Father knew himself in the Son made actual and visible and imitable. Christ and the Father are one, and for us, under the sanctifying action of the Holy Spirit, Christ is the way to the Father, the embodiment of truth, the perfection and source of life. Though all this may seem to go against our main thesis, namely that of simplicity, it is in fact a defense of simplicity. It is in fact the supreme justification of simplicity. As man contemplates the mysteries of divine love, his concepts become both clearer and more comprehensive. While the ways of God remain "unsearchable," and the mysteries remain as mysterious as ever, the man of prayer acquires a certain overall grasp which relieves him of searching too closely into the ways of God and of trying to work out his mysteries. It is this kind of person whom St. Paul has in mind when he prays that "out of his infinite glory he may give you the power through the Spirit for your hidden self to grow strong, so that Christ may live in your hearts by faith, and then, planted in love and built on love, you will with all the saints be able to comprehend the breadth and the length, the height and the depth, until, knowing the love of Christ, which is beyond all knowledge, you are filled with the utter fullness of God." Such a faith goes beyond all knowledge because it is not slowed down by the minutiae of knowledge.

Our apprehension of God tends therefore to become calmer, deeper, more intuitive. This is so whether we happen to be praying or not. The spontaneous reaction to the presence of God is comprehensive and direct. Thomas Aquinas says that the soul sees in creation "a certain cycle by which all beings return to the source from which they came, so that the first cause is also the end. All beings therefore must return to the end by the same causes in virtue of which they came from the source." This might be a commentary on the experience of Elias, as cited above, where the phrophet is told to go back the way he came. St. Thomas goes on: "And just as the procession of Persons is the reason for creation, so it is also the cause of our return to the end. It is by the Son and the Holy Spirit that we have to be created, and it is by them that we shall rejoin him who has made us."*

* In 1 Sent: Dist. XIV, Q. 2

5

Simplicity and Silence

When our Lord told the woman at the well in Samaria that those who worshipped truly did so "in spirit and in truth" he might equally have said that true worship was to be given in silence and sincerity. His words as they stand mean that prayer must come from the soul and not merely from the lips, and that it must be an honest and true expression of praise. "In spirit" implies conformity to grace; "in truth" implies conformity not only to what is in the mind of one praying but also to what has been revealed by the one to whom the prayer is offered. Such worship needs reflection, and reflection needs silence.

If truth, according to Pascal, can be made into an idol, so also can silence. But this does not excuse us from searching for truth in all things or from purifying our search with silence. Silence for silence's sake would be worthless, but silence for simplicity's sake and for prayer's sake is very valuable indeed. Without it there can be no supernatural simplicity and no deep prayer. There is today a great deal of talk about truth — more than in any other age on account of the communication media — but because there is less silence in which to think about truth the conclusions reached are fragmented. They are also for the most part unconvincing. When speculation is rife it is always better to go to truths you know and not to bother about the truths which other people think they know because they have just discovered them. A facet of truth newly appreciated can be so dazzling as to blind the well-intentioned searcher to the existence of all truth. Safer than making much of this or that aspect of truth, which nearly always is presented in opposition to established truth, would be to make for him who is truth itself. This is the way of simplicity, the way which values silence above talk. Silence is not much preached today, so it is for prayer to preach it. "Silence" says Heraclitus, "is a listening to the truth of things." If we do not listen we do not come to truth. If we do not pray we do not even get as far as listening. The four things go together: silence, listening, prayer, truth.

In a world wedded to noise, and among people who are afraid to stop and think, silence has become something which has to be extracted from the environment. Instead of silence being the natural habitat of the soul, as nature is the natural habitat of the body, it is now something which has to be arranged for. We have to make rules in order to secure it, and when secured it is something which has to be "kept", has to be safeguarded. To think of having to hire silence, as you would have to hire a cab in the street or time on the air, is distasteful but in an artificial society it has come to that. In a materialistic civilization the values which, through living naturally, were naturally respected as being given by God for man's guidance, are either ignored or reversed. Simplicity is one such value, silence is another.

When man is given over to what St. Paul calls a "reprobate sense" his judgements are turned inside out and he values the things of life without reference to the spirit. His criteria are either sensual, pragmatic, or purely rational. For him it is the expedient that counts. There is no money in silence, silence gets on his nerves, it is reasonable to talk and have the radio on all day.

Just as the simplicity of the child precedes the complexity of the man so silence pre-dates the invasion of sound. And if the act of creation came out from silence, so also did the incarnation. "Jesus, the Word that came forth out of silence" says Ignatius of Antioch. In the Christmas liturgy the refrain is repeated a number of times: "While deep silence held all things, and while the night was in the midst of its course, your almighty Word came out from royal thrones." The text, its opening words coming from the Book of Wisdom, shows us the positive role of silence. It is not only something which we for our part must preserve if we are to welcome the Word; it is something which preserves *us*. Silence here is thought of as "holding" all things in readiness, "keeping" creation prepared. The least we can do is to further this work by keeping silence ourselves, holding our souls in recollected readiness.

"Silences" observed Kierkegaard with characteristic exaggeration, "are the only scrap of Christianity we have left." Truths have to be presented forcefully, even overstrained, if they are to be listened to. If our Lord could tell his hearers that it would be easier for a camel to get though a needle's eye than for a rich man to enter heaven, an apostle of silence is within his rights when he identifies it with Christianity. Christ's life sets the pattern for silence: silence at the beginning in the cave; silence at the end in the tomb; long silences in between.

71

Goodness, says Aquinas, communicates itself. If the highest good is charity, and if the most perfect expression of charity is the contemplation of God, then contemplation communicates what has been listened to in silence. Silence, accordingly, is far from sterile: it gives birth to the twofold articulation of charity. It speaks to God on behalf of man, and to man on behalf of God. This silence moreover, judged as something spiritual and not as the mere absence of noise, reflects the simple silence and silent simplicity of God.

So the man of prayer, in looking for solitude and silence, is not trying to escape from people but trying to live in the presence of God. Those who accuse him of evading his responsibilities towards others have missed the whole point. He is neither hiding in a hole in the ground nor dreaming of a castle in the air: he is withdrawing from one kind of activity so as to devote himself more fully to another. He does not leave the needs of man out of account as being unworthy of his attention: he takes the needs of man with him into his solitude as being worthy of an attention which God alone can give. He is just as much committed to people as ever he was, but he is committed in a different way: he is not entangled. Because people played a part in Christ's life on earth, the man of prayer knows that people must play a part in his own life. If Christ is the way, the truth, the life for all, then people, since they are members of his body, must be for the man of prayer an inescapable part of the way, the truth, and life by which he comes to the Father. "No man comes to the Father but by me" says our Lord, and people are part of him. When charging the man of prayer with neglecting his obligations in the social and temporal order when he goes off into his silence, the critics are making the mistake of thinking that there has to be a clear-cut choice between God and people, and that the man who chooses God is choosing selfishly. The man who really chooses God knows well enough that the options are not mutually exclusive, and that in choosing God he is choosing people as well. People are a reality as God is a reality. It is just that God is the more important reality of the two. He finds the truth in God, and looks for it as reflected in people.

But even for this kind of argument to make sense, let alone to be practical in its implications, there has to be thought. There has to be time for thinking, and there has to be a solitude of sorts in which to do one's thinking. So back again at silence, and less directly at simplicity. We have to hollow out of what may be a noisy and variegated day enclaves of silence in which meditative reading as well as contemplative thought can be pursued without one eye on the clock and one ear on the telephone. Our proper element is the presence of God but our everyday element is the world. In God we "live and move and have our being" but in this world we happen to be.

If we are to live more fully, move more surely, enjoy a richer degree of being we must imitate God in his silence, simplicity, solitude. This in the practical field may mean retreats and days of recollection; certainly it will mean daily withdrawals into closed areas where sound, cares, and complications are left behind. Byron's Childe Harold is made to travel from country to country to escape, in vain as it turned out, his mental turmoil; we in this more psychiatric age know better than to attempt such a remedy. Geography does not solve psychological and spiritual problems. Our problems are far more likely to be met by securing a measure of silence and solitude than by any amount of change. Change only adds to our restlessness; silence lets us simmer down. If our minds are just as busy as the world outside our minds, the need for silence will be all the greater.

The world asserts itself through all the senses, but its power would be considerably reduced if it had to get through a barrier of silence before it could influence the particularly vulnerable senses of sight and touch. Silence gives just that pause which enables the soul to plan resistance. The impulsive response is halted, and the mood is changed from recklessness to that of reflection. If we had the sense to live constantly in a spirit of prayer, and so in a spirit of silence and simplicity, we would probably not sin at all. But because the world, the devil, and the flesh catch us on the hop, we are stampeded into giving consent to what, if we were educated in silence, we would not dream of accepting.

We who give ourselves airs about being followers of Christ are sometimes the worst offenders in the matter of silence and simplicity. We imagine that because we offer a shining example of external religious observance we are somehow immune from worldly contamination. Standing on our supposed mountain top we look down upon our less spiritual brethren who still, even in our advanced society, may well have need to practice such elementary things as silence, solitude, simplicity and so on. We congratulate ourselves upon having been trained in these traditional routines, but by now we feel we have grown out of them. But without the conditioned environment created by just these elements we are at the mercy of self-deception, false security, and pride. It is like the story of the Gadarene swine in reverse: the herd comes racing up the slope from the plain below and their devils enter into us without our knowing it. We would know it all right if we were more careful about our silence, solitude, and simplicity.

In a passage recounting an experience of God's presence, Augustine writes: "The tumult of the body was hushed,

hushed these shadows of earth, sea, sky; hushed the heavens and the soul itself. If all dreams were hushed and all sensuous emotions, and every tongue and every symbol; if all that comes and goes were hushed . . . suppose that they held this peace and turned their ear to him who made them, and that he alone spoke." Perhaps it is only the saints who can speak like this about silence without affectation. To the rest of us silence is at best a commodity and at worst an irksomeness. But silence is not something superinduced, something observed for the sake of discipline and good order, something which makes study easier, something which can serve as an excuse when tiresome people want to see us. Silence is something in its own right — with further reference to recollection. With further reference therefore to God himself.

If silence relates to God it relates to charity which is God. It relates not only to the charity which is the love of God but to the charity which is the love of neighbour. Stated baldly, we are united to one another not by talk but by charity. We are not necessarily united to one another by welfare work, but by the supernatural charity which inspires and informs the welfare work. All this is served in turn by silence. There is a difference between welfare work and the corporal works of mercy; still more between welfare work and the spiritual works of mercy. But it is only by means of prayer, which as we have seen supposes prayer and the single eye of simplicity, that this difference can be appreciated. The Christian's duty towards his neighbour is not fulfilled by providing schools, hospitals, recreation centres and soup kitchens. What it is in fact fulfilled by has to be learned from the Holy Spirit. The world can hardly be expected to believe that the union of charity can be effected without a single word being spoken.

If people are today forgetting about the eloquence of silence and are substituting the bombast of good works, they are forgetting also that the church's most telling apologetic is its simplicity and not its magnificence. Humility is far more likely to convert than fluency. Not many can have reached Christianity on waves of oratory. Are words and discussion groups worth more than silence and prayer? From bishops and theologians to journalists and television panelists we get plenty of controversy, Delphic guidance, ambigous and even contradictory instruction, idle conjecture and bewildering experiment . . . very little exhortation to silence and prayer, still less to poverty and repentance. Ecumenism, liturgical change, new theology, new understanding of scripture, are all very well but in what name are they preached and out of how much prayer and silence does the preaching come?

But even to its most ardent protagonists silence is not always an unmixed delight. As a discipline it can bring inconvenience, and as an experience it can bring loneliness. But the discipline, provided it is accepted and seen as part of one's prayer, cannot but be salutary; the experience, assuming that the loneliness does not drive one to despair, is one which normally accompanies the spiritual life. There is no denying that to be faithful to the regimen of silence may involve quite considerable, and in some cases quite heroic, struggles against depression. But then nobody ever pretended that safeguarding the life of prayer was going to be fun. A man's faults may, if he is not careful, flourish in the environment of silence. But this is where the formation of a truly spiritual character comes in. By the right use of silence and the other disciplines of the spiritual life, a new character takes the place of the old. Out of darkness comes light; out of longing for human companionship comes a desire to live in the company of God alone. Once again the Christian antiphon: "While the night was in the midst of its course, and all things were stilled in silence." Photographs are developed in a darkroom. Man's likeness to Christ is developed mostly in the dark in the process of waiting, in the enduring of certain processes which initially seem destructive. Solitude is far from amusing, but from the earliest ages of the church, when men and women fled into the desert to secure it, the silence of the cell or the pillar or the cave has been valued above the excellence of the social life. Human fellowship is good, but fellowship without silence to back it up and put it in its supernatural context is without merit.

Just as natural relationships take on spiritual character according to the degree of charity which is brought to bear upon them, so self denial is of spiritual value only in virtue of the charity with which it is performed. "Such exercises as fasting" says Thomas Merton, "cannot have their proper effect unless our motives for practicing them spring from personal meditation. We have to think what we are doing, and the reasons for our action must be enlivened by the transforming power of Christian love."* Without loss to the ideal of simplicity, and without having to make explicit acts every time we perform them, our self denials must be given direction or they remain neutral and of no spiritual significance. In fact without at least a virtual intention of making a prayer of our penances, ending up our sacrifices to God in union with the sacrifice of Calvary, we can all too easily use asceticism as a screen. Exterior penances can be paraded so as to hide the lack of interior self-denial. The purifying force of prayer is needed if self-denial is to be prevented from being show or purely routine. Far from diminishing the simplicity of self-denial performed in this way, the fact that it springs from prayer can only add to it. Where the spirit is simple, the acts which flow from that spirit will be simple.

* The Climate of Monastic Prayer, Irish University Press, p. 101

To some the idea that we have to have a pure intention in whatever we undertake is extremely daunting. It need not be. Given God's grace, which can always be counted upon, the habit of directing acts toward God is not so difficult to acquire. At first one has to remind oneself that the work in hand is more God's than one's own, but as the prayer life develops it becomes second nature to refer what one is doing to God. God is seen as the destination of all that is, as well as the prime mover and the first cause. To perform a work with a pure intention is not to superimpose something artificially and as it were by force; it is to allow the work to find its way simply and naturally towards its proper object which is God. The work accordingly follows the course set by prayer. In the life of prayer we pray not because of the instructions printed in the textbook to which our prayers must conform if they are to be blessed by God, but because we can now forget about the textbook and attend to God in simplicity and silence and truth. So also in the case of outward action: having found a prayerful way of acting we do not have to formulate the Godward intention every time we act. A person has to use a map when travelling in unfamiliar country, but once he knows he is moving in the right direction he can put away his map. Too many of us spend our prayer time studying the map so, of course, too many of us feel discouraged when told that a pure intention must accompany every step. The journey is not halted if we stop saying "I am on the right road, I am on the right road." If we sincerely want to be on the road which leads to God we *are* on the right road, and the movement towards him is not interrupted unless we change direction or deliberately slow down when we know we could be making a better pace.

A final consideration about simplicity and silence and simplicity in connection with joy. It is easy to see how simplicity makes for joy, less easy to see how silence does the same. The simple of heart are normally the most cheerful of people, but the silent have a name for being morose. The word "taciturn" which originally meant "given to silence" has come to mean disagreeable. Anyway unsociable. Yet if religious orders are anything to go by, and in questions of this sort they are a valid index, experience would seem to show that the more silent the order the more spirited its members. The reason for this is that their silence is super-naturalized. If their silence were compelled or self-willed or purely natural it would be cheerless. In the wrong sort of silence, superinduced and without the impulse of the spirit, souls will be found to go round and round on their troubles, phobias, and obsessions. Where silence, on the other hand, is orientated towards God it partakes of God's joy.

Ideally speaking, then, joy should result from a spirit of silence. Joy is a state of mind based on and emerging from virtues which grow in silence. Joy is not to be confused in this context with jolliness. As love is not benignity, joy is not gaiety. Though "God loves a cheerful giver" he will surely not be hard on those who are not by disposition cheerful but who make the most of the joy that comes their way. We shall not be blamed for being without joy, but we shall be blamed for missing it when it is offered. Joy is not an end in itself; it is a bonus, a by-product. It is something which is independent of outward circumstances. It is worth remembering that when St. Paul wrote to the Philippians "I want you to be happy, always happy in the Lord; I repeat, what I want is your happiness" he was writing from a prison cell. He goes on to tell the Philippians what must constitute their happiness: "The Lord is near; there is no need to worry, but if there is anything you need, pray for it, asking God for it with prayer and thanksgiving, and that peace of God which is so much greater than we can understand will guard your hearts and your thoughts in Christ Jesus."

If our silence does not bring the kind of joy St. Paul is talking about then there is something wrong with our silence. If we can find joy only in amusement then there is something wrong with our joy. The joy which spiritual people experience is the joy of which our Lord speaks in St. John's gospel. "I shall see you again" he says to his apostles on the last night which he spent with them, "and your hearts will be full of joy, and that joy no one shall take from you." Those who seem to be granted less than their fair share of joy in this life have nothing to worry about. In the silence of their prayer they can refer their joylessness to God, and he will give them just enough of it to get on with and at the same time will strengthen their hope. They will know, and perhaps know better than the habitually cheerful, where their true joy is to be found. Though it has not entered into the mind of man to know what great things God has prepared for those that love him, it should, by means of silently dwelling upon God's promises, enter into the mind of man to know that his joy will be to share eternally the joy of the risen Christ.

6

Life at Its Source

The intention of this book is to show that life is better left in God's hands than held in our own keeping — "the Lord rules me and I shall want for nothing" — and a chapter on the nature of human life in relation to God's providential scheme may help to confirm the idea. To imagine that by maneuvering the circumstances of our lives so that they will form a more satisfactory pattern than the one in which we find ourselves is a delusion from which we all suffer. We go to endless lengths to shift from an uncomfortable position into something which at last will give us a chance of serving God and finding happiness only to find ourselves worse off than we were before. A safer course is to say with the sacred writer "Lord, in the simplicity of my heart I have offered all to you", and then to leave him a free hand. If in the activity of prayer, as we have seen, the very natural and well-intentioned occupation of testing, winnowing, manipulating is a mistake, so also in the wider scene of ordinary life —

ordinary but lived on the momentum of prayer — the mistake is to pull strings. "Since the will of God must be the outcome anyway" the Jesuit brother Rodriguez is said to have observed, "I would rather it were done in me and by my consent than without me or by my effort to guide it." This is in effect the burden of these pages. But it should be easier to recognize the will of God as it manifests itself in my life if I recognize the will of God as it manifests itself in all life.

From what then does my life originate? Without going over the trodden ground of scientific controversy, creative evolution, biological reproduction and the rest of it, we can begin at the point in time when the animal brain took second place to the human intellect. Whether it was by instinct that the transformation was brought about — by the kind of instinct which turns bees and ants into social economists, beavers into builders and engineers, certain birds and snakes into experts in camouflage — or whether by the promotion of a particular species to lordship of creation, is not, in such a study as this, our concern. Our concern is with the action of God in the creation of the human soul in the pattern of creation. Nor is the pattern of creation to be thought of as a blueprint pinned upon a board but rather as the blueprint coming to life in the unrolling history of mankind. God's providential will is not something static, not a plan into which we must inescapably fit, but is a manifestation of his wisdom to which we can choose to respond or not respond. So skipping questions of natural selection, developing sensibility, environmental reaction, improved physical and psychological condition, hereditary influences — all the stock in trade of Darwinian evolution — we assume there to be a specific difference between the noblest beast and the most brute-like man, between the irrational and the rational animal, which no purely materialistic theory can explain and for which only this hypothesis is valid: God has given to man something of himself which has been denied to all other living creatures. In the scheme of creation man enjoys a prerogative which puts him above every other of God's handiwork: he possesses the faculty of reflective reason.

Where then do we, the individual persons living out our lives in this twentieth century, find a place in all this? The answer is that every separate human being finds his or her origin in the mind of God. Whatever our remote ancestors were before God breathed into them the living spirit, whatever the biological process by which their bodies were made ready for the infusion of a living soul, we personally are created each one unique. "As an intellectual creature" says Ronald Knox, "man is the *enfant terrible* of natural history, a cuckoo's egg in the nest of bewildered creation." The spiritual and the material are lined together in the individual who is myself. I am part animal but also part infinitely more. My dignity would have been assured even had there been no divine incarnation and redemption. With the life of Christ into which I am incorporated my natural dignity attains a new level; I am an adopted son of the Father, co-heir with Christ, and my destiny is to share this life in Christ for all eternity.

Once rational man abrogates his title to being lord of creation, irrational creation lords it over him. St. Thomas rates the intellect as the highest of God's gifts to man, but even this would not be a great help without the gift which puts the rational faculty to practical use. We have touched in passing upon the human will and the freedom of its exercise, but in even so unprofessional a survey of life's origins as this a closer look at the second of man's higher faculties is necessary. Men do not differ from beasts only because of a difference in intelligence: they differ because men have the power to put into operation, or to refuse to put into operation, what their intellect tells them. Animals, lacking the reasoning faculty, lack also the freedom to choose and to follow up their choice by practical application.

It could be argued that in certain circumstances man's will is so profoundly influenced as hardly to qualify as free. Is he on such occasions no better than the animal? Or take the man who for one reason or another — bad background, lack of moral formation, inherited weakness — would be described as not having a chance. Whether, as in the first case, moved by blind passion or, as in the second, conditioned to habitual wrongdoing, the human being cannot but act in accordance with his nature. His nature may be corrupt, his will may be overlaid by years of sinful choices, but so long as there is the slightest glimmer of conscience the will is capable of acting upon what the intellect tells him of the difference between right and wrong. Even if the will tries to stifle the thought of the alternatives presented, not only is the ultimate decision free but the decision to try to stifle the necessity of deciding is free. Where the animal has only instinct to guide its choices, man, however degraded, has a built-in sense of good and evil which makes him a responsible being. Diminished responsibility may justly be cited, but provided a man is capable of thought at all there cannot be an eliminated responsibility. A man may be bullied until he thinks he has no will of his own, may be subjected to torture so that his physical powers answer to another man's will, but for just as long as he remains conscious he possesses a will which is inalienable. Only when he loses his sanity, when he is no longer a rational being, does he lose his freedom of will. Even the subconscious has a will — which is perhaps a lot more free than we generally suppose it to be.

The trouble is that there are in us conflicting wills, conflicting motives and aims. St. Paul admitted that there was one law for his will and another law for his members "so that I do not the things that I will." This is our experience exactly: we have excellent intentions but poor performance. Sometimes we become so confused as not to know what our real intentions are. St. Augustine says that "a man is what he wills" and that it is his will which makes a man what he is. This should make for simplicity but in fact can induce a wasteful self-examination. But at least it is comforting to know that a man's true character is determined by his will rather than by his intellect. A man becomes what he chooses, not what he reasons. Reason gives him a knowledge of the many ways open to him; will gives him the momentum to go along one way rather than along another.

So complicated is the network of motives that it is best, for the sake of simplicity, to avoid sorting out any but the most obvious. Since in our intentions it is impossible to get rid of selfishness altogether, the wisest course is to face the humiliation of being a number of different selves at once when ideally speaking we should be straightforwardly one, to repudiate as sincerely as possible the less worthy intentions, and to refer the whole tangle to God. Above all to be avoided is making excuses for being what we are and for having such low motives and desires. This is tantamount to claiming a lack of freedom. We excuse our weaknesses by pretending that either invincible ignorance, duress, overpowering temptation, heredity, or (this worst of all) social pressure, has forced us to act in the way we do. The truth is that I am what I am in the sight of God, that he has made me a free agent, and that though all the world may reject Christ's standards it is still my business to follow his example and obey his law. I have been given the grace to walk freely in the way of the gospel, and only in attempting to follow this way can I find salvation.

"Whatever we are" says St. Augustine again, "we are not what we ought to be." Then there is St. Thomas who says that "every living organism tends towards its own proper perfection" Are they both saying the same thing, or is there some discrepancy here? You would think that we, as living organisms, should have progressed farther along the way towards our own proper perfection since the creation of the first man. That is precisely the trouble, and one wonders if the soul of modern man has not dropped lower than that of primitive man from the heights that could be gained in man's long history by all. On balance Cain does not come out too badly in comparison with the modern murderers whose methods include torture such as has not been equalled in the most barbarous periods of history. We of the twentieth century may have developed the intellect but we have shown ourselves markedly short on the will. God did not create man as a rational animal so that in the course of time a more inventive, technological — or even a sophisticated and cultured — being should emerge; he created man so that with reason and will he would be able to reflect and worship his own divine self.

Before the fall of man the human intellect and will worked in harmony as well as in subjection to the divine mind and will. With the fall came not only rebellion against God but disharmony within man. The imbalance of which the atrocities of today's so-called civilization are evidence could have been rectified when the second Adam came to atone for the first Adam's sin. The human will was given a second chance: a chance of carrying out what the human reason was given a chance of recognizing. But the Christian centuries have shown that the human reason has only partially accepted, and that in consequence the human will has only partially conformed. So that you get the situation now that Christian persecutes Christian, and that injustice, untruth, and immorality are as rife as ever they were before the coming of Christ. Christ, the Son of justice and love, surveys a world which could have taken on his ideal of justice and love but which has failed to do so, substituting a secular idea of justice and love. This secular understanding of justice and love inevitably breaks down when opposed beyond a certain point by human cupidity and human passion. The Christian safeguards are simply not there to restrain the animal side of man. When God made man human he did not prevent him from acting inhumanly. When Christ founded the Christian church he did not prevent Christians from acting in ways utterly unchristian. It is all a matter of what use a man makes of his opportunity. He is always free.

Anthropologists, biologists, and archaeologists can be helpful; philosophers and historians can be more helpful; only theologians and scripture scholars can provide us with the material which as Christians we really need here. We may feel inclined to agree with Rousseau in seeing his "noble savage" becoming less and less noble over the ages, but at the same time we must remember what theology and scripture tell us about the dignity of man and of the ability of man to climb with Christ to where, in a fallen world, he is meant to be. Man is not essentially corrupt, only potentially. A monster only by accident, destined, potentially and by grace, to be a saint.

In some ways, of course, man *has* advanced morally, and Christianity *has* had its leavening effect. There is, for instance, an increasing general concern about the distribution of the world's material products, about extending educational opportunity and supplying the needy with relief. All this represents a greater humanitarian awareness, but except in rare cases it has little to do with religion. The millenium cannot be achieved unless in addition to an awareness of human need there is also an awareness of God and sin; God to be worshipped, sin to be admitted and to be sorry for. Whatever acknowledgement there is of God and sin, whatever consciousness of responsibility, has not come into the world by accident or by intellectual evolution; it has come by grace. The religious sense is more than a culture; it is a gift. Even such humanitarian virtues as law and order were not promoted among men because they were found to be expedient in the running of society but because they answered to the instinctive knowledge of good and evil implanted by God in the heart of man.

So, however rebellious man may decide to be, he is by nature inclined to admit the claims of real authority. God has given him this inclination. However cynical he becomes about love, man cannot help allowing that there must be other aspects of it besides lust. However crudely a man may act, he would probably admit in his saner moments that kindness on the whole is a better bet. Bring to these natural, but partially suppressed, instincts the teaching of Christ, and you get obedience sanctified instead of merely necessitated; you get love explicitly defined in terms of charity instead of being dabbled in all anyhow; you get kindness, compassion, understanding forgiveness deliberately practiced in the name of Christ. You have the beatitudes bringing in a wholly new concept of morality which in turn leads to a wholly new appreciation of the relationship between the moral virtues and spirituality. You introduce the principle of the cross, the blessedness of voluntary poverty, the reversal of the valuations of the world. The gospel acceptations augment the good that has gone before and has only been waiting for the incarnation, and at the same time re-interpret human values to man. From now on it is not the successful who are to be envied but the unsuccessful; no question now of the survival of the fittest but instead the survival, in eternity, of the unfittest; not to be pitied are the mourners, the oppressed, the deprived, the ridiculed, the weak and the foolish, for in the long run they are to come off best.

The evolutionist is not the right man to explain these New Testament concepts: he has nothing but matter to work on. Nor is the agnostic philosopher any better qualified: he may be able to put the mind under the microscope but his findings have only an accidental bearing upon matters of the soul. The only one who is well placed to preach the significance of the gospel tenets is the practicing Christian, and woe to him if he fails to do so. We Christians who know what life is all about, who know that life on one plane must be denied if it is to be discovered on another, who know that the cross is not a negation but a liberation, can be lamentably silent on these subjects. Perhaps this is because we know them only as subjects to which we gave assent and not as principles of life. Not until principles of life have been allowed to pass from the intellect to the will – in other words, not until they have been made actual in personal experience – can they transform for us and for others with whom we share them, the whole world.

The wound to mankind left by original sin has never properly healed. Despite the restoration in Christ the scar-tissue remains. We can now leave the subject of original sin for a lengthy consideration of actual sin. We commit sin when consciously and deliberately we violate God's law or, more subtly, when we fail to respond to the summons of his will. St. Thomas says of law that it is "a certain ordinance of reason promulgated by one who is responsible for the common good." The supreme authority responsible for the common good is God but he communicates his authority to man for promulgation. "You would not have any authority over me" Christ said to Pilate, "unless it were given you by my Father." So, whether the authority is expressed directly (as in the commandments) or indirectly (through the church or the state or a person), the definition holds good. In its wider connotation, law has come to mean a principle which produces an invariable, or supposedly invariable, effect: the law of diminished returns, Parkinson's law, the law of averages, and so on. This second kind of law amplifies that first by analogy: it does not command or forbid but tells you what will happen if you break it.

We have seen above that every species must be true to its proper nature and must tend towards its own proper perfection. We are to see now how being false to one's nature can be to break the super-natural as well as the natural law. In the world's view this is all a lot of nonsense. The worldling, if he thinks about sin at all, judges these distinctions to be purely academic. He ignores them and thinks of moral lapses only in so far as they affect the social order. "Provided I don't harm anyone" is his rule and what he does in private is nobody's business but his own. This is utterly false but widely believed. It means that he has appointed himself the sole judge of moral action and is the jury as well; he does not see himself in the dock. Just as common a fallacy is "It is happening all the time, everyone does it now." The error here is twofold: firstly it supposes that the malice of sin is dependent upon a majority vote and not upon God's word; secondly it tries, by lessening guilt, to lessen the freedom of the will. The everyone-does-it attitude overrides the fact that every man has an individual destiny and acts on the wholly false proposition that man is conditioned by forces outside himself, chief among which is that which impels the average man to act in given circumstances as other average men happen to be acting. Out of this fallacy comes the "situation ethic" which allows the breaking of law when the circumstances are judged to be strong enough to demand it. This system, if it does not do away with the necessity of law altogether, refuses to admit that a rightly ordered conscience is one which is informed by law and not one which feels authorized to do without it. The principle of situation ethics rationalizes sin both in relation to God and in relation to law. Law in this view can *mis*inform conscience where it should be informing it.

It is significant that while in our virtually non-believing society the malice of sin tends to be overlooked, the sense of guilt is stronger than ever. Psychiatrists tell us that almost all neuroses spring from either guilt or fear. Modern man, for all his scorn of sin as such, is more guilt-ridden than his ancestors. The heinousness of sin as an offense against God is obviously more real to believers than to non-believers — the believer being therefore more culpable — but this does not let out the agnostic sinner, who, whatever way you look at it, sins against society (even in his solitary sins), against his own nature, against what still must remain the common conscience however many people go against it. The believer who leaves God out of his calculations is a rebel against God's love; against God's order. The sinner cannot win, and if he is honest with himself, he knows it.

7

Life in Maturity

Fashions in prejudice change almost as often as fashions in clothes. At one time it was the fashion to take a cynical view of enthusiasm, and if you wanted to be unkind about someone you said he was keen. Then the cry was raised against regimentation and conformism, so that anything which had to do with "establishment" came in for criticism. At the time of writing, the most popular sneer is to charge a person with immaturity. The phrase "drop dead" which one used to hear so often that he wanted to scream has been replaced by "grow up." One still wants to scream. Given half a chance the mind grows up of its own accord and the less it is forced to do so the better. The pace is not the same for all, and the degree reached is not the same for all, but there is good sense in wanting to mature as there is bad sense in wanting to hide behind a screen of immaturity. While the immaturity possesses certain advantages for those of lazy disposition, it can be a snare. If out of fear or selfconsciousness or false humility I refuse to move on and take my place among men I am asking to live a life deprived. I may tell myself I am playing safe, am seeking the shelter of a blameless conscience, am preferring a known security to the risk of losing my peace and possibly my soul, but I must also know that in the plan of God there is just as much risk in sitting with my eyes shut in the nursery when I am wanted for work with the grown-ups downstairs. If the unborn baby hugs the warmth and security of the womb beyond its time, it dies.

After all that has been said earlier about the blessedness of a childlike attitude towards life, it might seem contradictory to push the claims of maturity. The point to be made here is that the two are not exclusive, or even complimentary, but rather that true maturity reaches back, through experience, to the trust and simplicity of childhood. The mature man, integrated by reason of his increased likeness to Christ, becomes, in Christ, more positively the child of God. The Christian is by baptism incorporated into Christ's life, and by progressively modelling his life on the pattern presented by Christ, reverts to his baptismal state. He may be an adult when he is baptised but only when he has allowed his life to take the shape of Christ's life does he, in St. Paul's words, "reach full stature in Christ." Then is he a mature person. "The consequences of the mysteries of the faith are my perfection" says St. Gregory Nazianzen, "are my restoration, are my return to the innocence of the first Adam." Christian maturity then is passing through adult experience with all its dissipated energy and fragmented impressions to the integrity of childhood. The mature Christian arrives at a one-ness of spirit and a knowledge that he is loved by God. Where hitherto the phrase "God loves me" was a proposition he vaguely knew was true, now it is a certainty which he knows from the inside. "A man passes from adolescence to maturity" writes Dr. Odier, "with a sense of autonomy, a feeling of interior value." A sense, it might be added, of exterior value as well. The truly integrated individual who is centred on his religion is able to distinguish between what is important in God's eyes and what is not. He is able to see that his own peace comes from the peace of God, and that his own sufferings find their place in the passion of Christ. Interior and exterior circumstances are viewed in unity.

Have we not all come across people, grown men and women, who remain on the fringe of life and seem quite content to stay there? They are familiar with the ways of the world, well informed, cultured, authorities perhaps on this and that, yet their lives seem never properly to have set. They are not conscious of lacking anything. On the contrary they often appear to be all too satisfied with what they have found. But what have they found? They have not found either man's true place in the scheme of creation nor, more immediately, their own. They can jog along with their amusements, can meet their troubles more or less philosophically, can manage to get by without going deeply into ends and origins. Passing satisfactions compensate for passing disappointments. But is this good enough? Surely the first lesson of the growing mind is that there must be more in life than would appear on the surface, and that if persons are to be complete beings they must discover what it is. Otherwise they are like children who skim through the book, looking only at the pictures lest they come upon long words which they will not understand. A grown-up person ought to understand, ought to know what he is supposed to be developing into and why. His life should have shape, direction, and destination. Even at this present-day stage in the evolution of the human intelligence there are many who, believing that man is in fact developing, are not at all clear as to the rationale of this development or the goal aimed at.

If we believe in the wisdom of God we must believe that creation moves according to a providential plan and that the end of the world can come about only when mankind has developed to a point of maturity preordained by God. If nature's movement towards maturity is purposeful and not arbitrary, Christianity's is no less so. Nor is this a matter for the world seen in terms of the human race, or for the church seen as all believers: the pull towards maturity is designed by God to attract every single member of the human race, every separate single soul made in the image of God. When the time comes for the Eternal Father to lock all doors save the one at the entrance of heaven, he may find that charity on earth has grown cold and that the faith is being held by only a few, but as far as you and I are concerned the summons to the perfection of charity and faith remains the same. The thought that the human race has a long way to go is daunting enough, the thought that we as individuals have got to climb our way to the degree of perfection God is demanding of us is even less encouraging. At the present rate of progress there would seem to be no hope, but this is exactly where trust must be brought to bear.

A man ought to be able to say: "I am a Christian and I belong to a living church. I am growing up with my church and may not stagnate. The similes of the New Testament — the vine, the body, the seed, the leaven — teach growth. If I become as a fly encased in amber I may preserve a certain immunity but actually I am opting out." In urging people to leave their lives alone we do not mean that on the one hand they must let the world go by or on the other that they may drift casually wherever it leads. We are urging them to take up life with both hands but to let God control it. Not to fuss about it. Not to compare it with the more agreeable lives of others. Not to go on and on about how much better our service of God would be if we were not handicapped by bad health, lack of money, lack of opportunity. All this is childishness, immaturity. It means we are looking at ourselves and not at God; we are forgetting that there is any sort of providential plan about our life and imagining that God would not only have made us happier but would have served his own interests better had he taken more care over its setting. We should have the generosity to admit that within our appointed setting God leaves us plenty of room to live out our lives in a blending of our will with his. Even if he does not always grant their fulfilment he allows us our hopes and dreams. Without them we would not be able to get along at all. Some of them may even be a prelude to their realization — provided always his claims come first. Fulfilling a desire which we share with him is perhaps our way of achieving maturity. But it will not be a short cut, not by bringing in his will as an afterthought. It will be by first learning his will and then making it our own.

One of the factors which may well delay the reaching of true maturity is the way in which the pace of modern life forces people to a premature and therefore unreal maturity. Changes in the social and moral patterns follow one another so fast that in order to keep up there have to be psychological adjustments which not everyone can make. A degree of disorientation is inevitable in times of rapid transition, but the disorientation which is everywhere evident in our society is quite unlike anything that has ever happened before and man has therefore no precedent in dealing with it. It is a case of progress having a retarding effect. Man is advancing too quickly — backwards. This is what an authority and contemporary observer, Mr. Alvin Toffler, calls "future shock," and from what he has to say about it one can only judge that true maturity will from now onwards be harder to attain to than ever. "Future shock" he says "arises from the superimposition of a new culture on an old one. It is a culture shock in one's own society. But its impact is far worse. For most travellers have the comforting knowledge that the culture they left will be there to return to. The victim of future shock does not." Mr. Toffler's warning conclusion is that we have released a whole category of new social and technological forces without weighing up their consequences, and that unless we find a way of controlling them they will run us off our feet. The signs are already there to suggest that he may be only too right: mass neurosis, violence, lack of restraint, race hatred. Wine cannot mature on a vibrating factory floor, nor can the human psyche reach vintage quality when under pressures which it was never designed — anyway all at once — to meet.

As a result of this speedy turnover human beings at both ends of age-grouping are the chief sufferers. Children in recent years reach so-called maturity at an alarmingly early age while old people retreat from their mature responsibilities and ways long before they need to. The condition at both ends of the scale is artificially induced and therefore unnatural. The little boy of eight who puts on a false beard to play cops and robbers is none the worse for it, but if you cause him to grow a real beard at that age you are storing up trouble for everybody. No less unreal is the tendency among the old to adopt the "stop the world I want to get off" attitude towards life. But you can hardly blame them. To anyone over the age of about fifty the idiom of the young is difficult to understand and their anarchism even more so. Manners, customs, tastes in music and art and drama have so much changed among younger adults as to make the elderly feel more out of things than ever, and lonely. So they shut off their brains, withdraw their sympathy, put on their slippers and stare sadly at the ceiling. We may think it silly for old women to dress like high school students but we should think it serious when they no longer want to. When a revolution takes place, and wins hands down, it is not much fun for those who are left on the losing side.

Yet in the midst of all this social, religious, educational confusion it must still be possible for us to preserve our integrity or God would not have placed us in the present set up. Each generation, each individual, is given the appropriate grace to deal with the existing provocation. We may be dismayed at the turn civilization has taken, we may loathe this nylon-fabricated, candy-coated, soft-centred, flourescent-lit, plastic-packed culture but we should take heart in the thought that it is not happening behind God's back, or because he has ceased to interest himself in the true progress of his world. A civilization does not come about by chance: it is the civilization we deserve. It reflects the current mood, the inward thought. From the point of view of the service it renders to God it may be an unfortunate manifestation but inevitably it must be one permitted by God, and one in which the individual soul can find his God-given place. To a soul of another age, past or future, our present environment might be utterly disastrous. But it cannot be so to us or we would not be existing now. In the context of the present each of us is able to reach maturity.

So it comes down to this: we are always free to preserve our integrity wherever we are and whenever we live. In one of her poems Emily Bronte says:

> Often rebuked, yet always back returning
> To those first feelings that were born with me...
> I'll walk but not in old heroic traces,
> And not in paths of high morality,
> And not among the half distinguished faces,
> The clouded forms of long-past history,
> I'll walk where my own nature would be leading;
> It vexes me to choose another guide.

The mistake is trying to walk in heroic traces which do not belong to the age in which God has set me, trying to number myself among the half-distinguished faces of another time. I have, lying at hand, the full apparatus for either self-perfection or self-destruction, the only difference between the present and the "clouded forms of long-past history" being that where at one time there was breathing space to ponder and decide, today the area of debate is so narrowed as almost – or this is what it seems – to take the decision out of my hand.

There can be confusion of thought in this matter of maturity. Maturity need not necessarily go with being a man or woman of the world. The saints are the mature people, and they are certainly not men and women of the world. There is this about maturity – that it does not go with putting on an act. The moment a person pretends to be what he is not, he is nothing. The saints did not pretend; so they were simple, so they were mature.

Most of us are pretending for a large part of the day so that when we are not we are unsure about what we really are. We pretend to be important, to be strong minded, to be experienced, to be above such ignoble things as jealousy, class-consciousness, desire for attention. But this is all a fiction, and none of it is any good because it is neither true, simple, mature, or God directed. Maturity is being nearer to God; importance and recognition are nearer to self. What is the use of being recognized for something which we are not? Even having a good practical judgement is not necessarily to be mature. Maturity is having a judgement informed by grace and God's law — which is not at all the same thing. There are occasions when a practical judgement leads to opportunism; a mature judgement, anyway for the Christian, waits upon the wisdom of God.

Essential to maturity then is a sufficient rising above pose which enables a man spontaneously to express his own nature to the full. It is frank perception of the person he really is and of his ability, by God's grace, to maintain that identity. It is not, in the terms of the Karl Jaspers quotation printed at the beginning of this book, the man's "moulding of his own life into completeness" but rather the handing of his own life over to the life of God for moulding. Since the life of God is expressed for us in the life of Christ, the moulding to which the mature Christian submits himself will assume, as a major part of the process, the cross. The element of suffering in the Christian's growing up is not a fortuitous circumstance. It is not accidental but essential. The serious Christian does not opt for suffering or leave it out according to temperament and attraction: it will be there in his life whether he feels spiritually drawn to it or not. It is not only an ideal but a datum. For Christian perfection it is a sine qua non, and one ventures to think that even as regards psychological stature the bitter experience of sorrow and rejection must be part of the training. Outward defeat, inward sense of failure: maturity is the phoenix.

So spiritual maturity shows itself in the ability to transcend not only repeated frustrations but the mood of despair which repeated frustrations can engender. The spiritually mature are not impervious to disappointment, but are perhaps more keenly sensitive to it than most. The point is that they are not governed by it, do not sink into self-pity because of it, are not fatalistic about it. They accept the cross and even, without being morbid or superstitious about it, expect the cross; they do not make it their whole preoccupation. With an awareness of Christ's promise about the yoke being sweet and the burden light when endured with him, Christian sufferers aim as far as possible at self-forgetfulness in their sufferings. The protesting self, the resentful and potentially embittered self, will be silenced. The reaction to every trial will be St. Paul's "I have learned in whatsoever state I am to be content therewith." Such an attitude is a degree of personal fulfilment not often attained by men and women of considerable ability and position. In an age when achievement counts for more than motive, efficiency is often mistaken for maturity. Achievement is not the lot of all, so the Christian would be wise to cultivate the disposition of being content to do without it.

The integrated man, who looks at the world with adult eyes, is able to say: "This is where I belong, and this is the time which belongs to me to use or misuse. I am a member of a clan which has grown up with me and from which I have much to learn. I have need primarily to lean on God but I shall need, too, the support of my fellow men. If I think myself to be above others in experience and maturity, I am, in fact, below them and have not even begun to live. There is no fulness of life without humility, and there is no humility that is not taught of God."

There was once a student of philosophy who gave himself great airs as a man of knowledge and sophistication. When asked on one occasion to give the definition of a joke he weighed in with an introductory lecture on the distinction between wit and humour. "Yes, but how would you define a joke?" his questioner pressed him. "For a joke to satisfy the requirements" explained the philosopher, "there have to be present two elements: contrast and surprise. Thus when an illiterate indigent or tramp is shown as a shrewd social commentator, or when an animal — say an elephant — voices a rational opinion the effect is generally droll; but on the other hand — " ... At this point a small boy came into the room. To the interrogator this came as a welcome distraction from a monologue which threatened to be of some length. "Well, let's have your opinion" he said to the little boy, "what do *you* think a joke is?" "It's something" was the prompt reply, "which makes you go *ha, ha.*"

If simplicity and humility go a long way towards forming a soul in maturity, peace and joy are very often its accompaniment. Our Lord promised to his followers a peace which the world could not give and told them to pray for what they wanted so that their joy might be full. The implication is that his true disciples, complete Christians, should be men of serenity and need have no scruple about asking for whatever is likely to further it. "Peace I *leave* with you, my peace I *give* to you ... these things I have spoken to you that in me you may have peace." St. Paul says that "Christ came and *preached* peace ... God has *called* us to peace ... let the God of peace rule in your hearts, sanctify you wholly ... may God fill you with all joy and peace in believing." It is worth noting that our Lord preached peace more often in Jerusalem which was disturbed than in rural Galilee which was quiet. The suggestion here is that peace comes not by establishing a calm outward setting so much as by inwardly surrendering to whatever the setting. "I do not want the peace you find in a stone" said Gandhi whose doctrine had mainly to do with what he called the "truth force."

Where the materialist pursues peace relentlessly and along all the wrong avenues, the mature Christian does not pursue it as an end but enjoys it without thinking too much about it. He *finds* it. The *daemon* of anxiety so shadows the materialist that he dare not sit down and rest in the peace which is waiting for him if only he would take it from God's hands. He trusts in tranquilizers and is then surprised at finding his inward conflicts still unsolved. In the play *Period of Adjustment* Tennessee Williams shows us a suburb which sprawls uneasily over a stretch of hollow ground. Building on the wrong foundations the materialist is subject to a process of subsidence which gathers momentum the more weight he puts on it. If peace is not to be found in a cavern, it is certainly not to be found on the shifting soil which covers it.

Joy is the same way. If love is not merely being good-natured or romantic or sensual, and if peace is not merely being placid or drugged or uninvolved, then joy is not merely being jolly. There is no beatitude which says "Blessed are the jovial for they shall keep up their spirits." Instead there is the sobering beatitude "Blessed are they that mourn." But mourning and joy are not opposites. The opposite of joy is not gloom but disillusion. The opposite of mourning is not celebrating but despairing. Joy and trust go together; joy and pleasure not necessarily; joy and sensation hardly ever.

Perhaps inherited from the days of the British Empire is the tendency to think of the mature man as strong, cool, and silent. This the mature man may be but it will not be in virtue of his Christianity. It will be largely because of Dr. Arnold. When our Lord said "learn of me because I am gentle and lowly of heart" he was clearly not thinking of what must go into building our kind of empire. He said exactly what kind of empire he was establishing: "my kingdom is not of this world . . . blessed are the poor in spirit for theirs is the kingdom of heaven . . . whoever humbles himself like this child, he is the greatest in the kingdom of heaven." To show how different his kind of kingdom was to be from the kind the world thinks of, he entrusted its keys to a fisherman. St. Peter was by nature neither strong, nor cool, nor silent.

The important thing about St. Peter was that from first to last he was himself, and that on account of this native simplicity the Holy Spirit had something sure to work upon. Had St. Peter been thinking of his image and not of Christ he would have made even more mistakes than he did and would have gone on being immature, not to be relied upon and ready to say the first thing that came into his head, for the rest of his life. Instead, while retaining his own sharply defined personality, he was able to grow out of his *volte face* inclinations and the mood in which he would slice off someone's ear. It would seem to be an invariable law in the development of sanctity that a man remains faithful to himself in being faithful to God. Grace does not break down the personality into small pieces and then substitute something out of a different mould. Grace works upon the wholeness of the person and the person emerges whole and purified, identified with Christ. In an interview with Timothy Wilson as printed by way of introduction to his book *School of Prayer*, Archbishop Bloom said this: "I never ask myself what the result of any action will be — that is God's concern. The only question I keep asking myself in life is: what should I do at this particular moment? What should I say? All you can do is to be at every single moment as true as you can with all the power of your being — and then leave it to God to use you, even despite yourself." There are those who claim that people never know whether their acts are right or wrong until ten years after they have acted. Right or wrong, truth or untruth, cannot depend upon results ten years or ten minutes after acting. What should I do at this particular moment? This is the only question that matters. Archbishop Bloom gets as near as anybody does to the answer.

8

Adaptation to Life

There is a kind of adaptability which the soul of prayer needs to consider. This kind is concerned not with the desire for change but with detachment in the face of change. Assuming that change has, whether legitimately or fortuitously, come about, there is no limit to the soul's opportunity. When all has been done that could be done to resist what was thought to be an abuse of liberty, the course to follow now is that of complete submission to the providential will of God. "I will praise the Lord at all times" says the psalmist; not only when the times are going my way. Just as the wrong sort of flexibility comes of weakness and worldliness, the right sort comes of hair-trigger response to the movement of grace. Our ideal here is the receptivity shown by our Lady on receiving the message from Gabriel: she scrapped whatever ideas she may have had regarding the future and the service of God to which she felt drawn, and accepted with wholehearted consent the vocation to which

God was in fact calling her. Good people, with their good intentions mapped out in front of them, often make the mistake of sticking rigidly to the programme when God is calling them to a different expression of service. Fidelity to the plan has to be carefully looked at in case it is no more than obstinacy.

It was said after the war that the difference between the German campaigns in North Africa and ours was that Rommel planned his strategy from a ball of string while our generals planned from a coil of wire. Certainly in religious matters the wire of twenty years ago, or even of ten, has given place to the string and, with qualifications that are obvious, this is all to the good. We make our dispositions according to the necessity of the moment. But let it be the God-given moment and not the moment of our own choosing. Or take the illustration from the parachute which has to be made of silk or nylon. If it were made of three-ply wood or even plastic it would not be able to yield to the wind or open out when dropped from the plane. These examples never quite match the spiritual situation because the soul's flexibility under the impulse of grace is itself a grace. It would be as though the string were moving by a power of its own and the parachute were the same as the wind which filled it.

What we forget is that such good as we find within ourselves is not of our own making but of grace. St. Paul says we cannot even call upon the Lord's name unless God gives us the impulse and power to do so. We do not act virtuously because we are strongminded or amiable but because God is acting in us. Every virtue is an aspect of charity, and charity is God. "He who lives in charity lives in God, and God in him." Our charity is God living in us and working in and through the unpromising material which is us. It is like a lily pushing its way into the open through a rubbish dump. The notion surprises us because we are not used to thinking of ourselves as a rubbish dump but as a garden of lilies.

If we could adapt ourselves more to the life of God within us we would be more able to adapt ourselves to the will of God as expressed all about us. We are unyielding in outward things only because we have not fully yielded to inward ones. The integrated soul, the man who has broken down the barriers of selfishness and is detached from his own will, is ready to meet every circumstance however suddenly presented and however apparently destructive, fortuitous, unreasonable, and mad.

There is a story in the *Talmud* which tells of a certain rabbi and his wife who had two sons to whom they were very much devoted. On the morning of one sabbath day, while the rabbi was out teaching the Law, both boys were struck by a sudden illness and died. Their mother laid them on a bed and covered them with a sheet. When the rabbi came home for his meal and asked where the children were, his wife made some excuse and waited until the rabbi had eaten. She did not answer his question but in her turn asked one of him. "I am placed in a difficulty" she said, "because some time ago a person entrusted to my care some possessions of great value which he now wants me to give back. Am I obliged to do this?" "That you should need to put this question surprises me" the rabbi replied, "since there can be no doubt. How can you hesitate to restore to everyone his own?" His wife then took the rabbi back to the room where the two bodies lay and pulled back the sheet. "My sons, my sons," groaned the father in his pain. "The Lord gave, and the Lord has taken away" said his wife through her tears, "and you have taught me to restore without reluctance that which has been lent to us for our happiness."

Leave Your Life Alone

Another Hebraic story which teaches the same doctrine of detachment is about two young men who asked their master to comment on the words of the Mishnah: "A man must bless God for the bad in the way that he blesses him for the good that befalls." Their master directed them to the house of the Rabbi Zusya who would give them the best explanation. When asked, the Rabbi Zusya laughed and said: "I am surprised that you were sent to me. Go to another, and this time choose a man who has suffered tribulations. As for me, I have experienced only good things all my days." When the two students learned how the Rabbi Zusya had from his earliest hours to the present endured the deepest sorrows and afflictions they knew why they had been sent to him.

Afflictions may deprive a man but only sin diminishes him. A man need never be destroyed against his will, and though he may feel defeated by a particular trial or by life itself — the sheer burden of having to live and the too-muchness of it — he may in God's sight be resisting defeat and even triumphing over it. Nothing in life can ever prevent him from repeating the psalmist's determination to "praise the Lord at all times", however bad the times may be. A man does not have to wait for better days in which it will be possible to praise the Lord; he can praise the Lord just as well, indeed more effectively, on days that are worse. When his spirits are at their lowest there is nothing to prevent his trust being at its highest. He must be detached from his spirits, which is only another word for his moods, and attached only to God.

Much harder than being detached from comforts and possessions is being detached from one's dreams of happiness, from one's hopes for a temporal solution to one's difficulties, from one's accustomed ways of serving God. Nothing must weigh in the balance against the will of God. Not that there need be anything wrong in wishing that this or that would happen and so bring relief — hopes of this kind are often a prelude to realization and may themselves bring temporary relief — but the wishing must be subject to what God may will. Detachment means nothing if it does not mean this.

Adaptation, then, goes deeper than accepting as the will of God the times in which we live, and which we may detest; deeper than accepting the people with whom we have to deal, and whom we find antipathetic; it means accepting ourselves whom we heartily despise. We may dislike our work, our surroundings, the policy of those who rule our lives, but whatever it costs us we can usually manage to see God's will in these things. Where it is harder to see God's will is in our own continued insufficiency. We have to be detached not only from the petty shortcomings which in others we find contemptible and in ourselves exaggerated, but from the more serious weaknesses in our character which we seem incapable of correcting. There comes a time in more or less good people's lives when they would give anything to be someone else. Anyone else. They are disgusted at not having made a better showing before God whom they had set out to serve in full perfection. What other people think of them does not matter any more. It is in the sight of God that their own inconsistency, hypocrisy, timidity, sensuality, self-pity, uncharity mount up to such a glaring infidelity. To think of their lives as being to the glory of God is laughable. They see all this and at the same time know that they lack the strength of will to do anything about it. How else can humility be learned if not from the inside? Only now, with the evidence of failure all along the line, can we drop the pretences which have kept our ego comfortably bolstered. Indeed we are forced to. There is nothing to depend upon now but the sheer mercy of God.

St. Bernard says that man needs to show charity towards God, towards his neighbour, and towards himself. Of the three the third can be the hardest to practice. In the condition of soul considered above, a soul finds it easier to respond to God's love in terms of love, and to show tolerance towards others, than to accept oneself as one is. Yet adaptation to life, whether it is God's life as revealed in his will or man's life as affecting one's own or the life as experienced by me the individual, is an aspect of charity. Nobody may be excluded from my charity, not even myself. Charity in its every aspect demands detachment, and in this particular aspect the demand, provided it is not made an excuse for spinelessness, is only that patience and forbearance should be taken one step farther than is normally felt to be necessary. I take myself as I am until God chooses to make me into someone better — either in this life or in the next. To change other people might be in my power if I were arrogant enough to attempt it; to change myself is something for which I would need a miracle of grace. I can hopefully await this miracle, but if no miracle is granted I can go on waiting upon the grace of God from day to day. The title of this book has not been lightly chosen.

The great thing *now* to avoid is having a grudge against the way life has treated you and against the world, because if this is allowed the least scope it ends up with a grudge against God. Then the whole process, which was designed to be so purifying, is wasted. You may expect great things of life, but it is of the first importance not to think that life *owes* you anything. Life owes you nothing but what you can give yourself. Half the convicted criminals, and probably all suicides, are those who imagine that they have claims which life has not met. With some it is a grudge against society, with others against individuals, with others against themselves. In one way or another life has cheated them and they mean to compensate. Even taking your own life is an assertion of rights — a last slap in the face of life for having denied what was thought to be owing.

The spirit of God is never in disillusion over the things of God. God's providence may ask for our crushing disappointment — frequently does — but the disappointment is only as crushing as we allow it to be. It may spark off a desire for revenge but this need be no more than a nervous reaction. The idea behind every disappointment is resignation. Repeated disappointments are meant to make people flexible, not hard. Adaptability again — to every new situation. Though crime and suicide may be attributable to lack of resignation, so also are other forms of escape such as drink, drugs, refusal in one way or another to face the duty of living. The more man tries to people the emptiness with false gods the more he feels the need to get out of it altogether. But if society cannot show its members the way, and if the way of the gospel has been rejected, there is nothing for the members to do but form their own little individual cells within society, and in so doing to create their own little personal voids. The result is loneliness, fear to adjust, opting out.

But unfortunately you cannot opt out from yourself. It is like those wooden dolls (Dutch? Swiss? German?) which unscrew in the middle to reveal another, and so on until you have a line of dolls which ends up with one so small that it cannot be unscrewed. The points to note about the painted wooden dolls are that each of them except the last is hollow, and that though identical in design they diminish as they leave the prototype. The last one has no more hollows in which to hide, but by this time it is so diminished that it hardly qualifies as a doll at all. It may not be hollow but it is separated from its own kind.

Civilization as it is today conduces to one of the things it most wants to avoid: alienation. Though refusal to adapt to the existing order can account for substituting *dis*order, there is another escape to which this resentment against life can give rise: the search for a solitude which is blessed neither by God nor nature. The little painted doll at the end of the line is the self-contained isolationist. Nature and grace work from the inside out, not from the outside in. The silkworm does not begin as a butterfly and end up as a chrysalis safely wrapped around in its cocoon; man, created gregarious, is not meant to end up between sandwich-boards which say "Do not disturb." Ideally speaking, the Christian, taking to heart the gospel message of hope, should be optimistic in outlook, but if he cannot manage that, and it may not be his fault that he cannot, he must know that it is not by the drawing of grace that he becomes misanthropic.

Society is not made by governments but by the drift of its individual members. "What would present-day society be like" we can ask, "if all its members were like me?" If I shut myself off in my separatist life, and if my neighbour does the same, not only do I cease to be a neighbour to the man next door but he and I together are contributing to a separatist society. It is easy to see how our modern society is poisoned — whatever it professes in the name of democracy — by racial discrimination, nationalism, class distinction, religious and economic segregation. It is less easy to see our guilt in this, less easy still to admit it and do something about it.

If the standards of the community are the standards of its subjects the same is, of course, true of the church and its individual faithful. We talk a lot about ecumenism and Christian unity but if in our lives we keep people at a distance we are getting in the way of those ideals. The enemy of unity in religion is not sectarian bigotry but lack of cohesion nearer home. If there is a law of diminished returns there is also a law of increased alienation: independence and isolation accelerate disunity every bit as effectively as denominational prejudice.

We either believe in the providence of God or we do not. If we do not believe in it there is no problem: chance rules the day. But given belief in the existence of a divine plan which comes from the mind of absolute wisdom the subtleties of obedience to it become finer and finer as by the light of prayer we may come to see more of it. For example, it is related of a holy man that while walking on the beach one evening with his friends he picked up a grain of sand, looked at it closely, and put it back as nearly as possible from where it came. "Why did you do that?" one of his disciples asked. "He who does not believe that God wants this bit of sand to lie in the place where I found it" replied the holy man, "does not believe at all."

There is a danger of exaggeration here which could lead to determinism. There is a whiff of pre-destination about seeing everything as written in the stars. Different people understand the working of providence in different ways but to understand it in the orthodox sense there has to be a closer connection with the wisdom of God than with the stars. "It was meant" is one way of looking at the contingencies of life, and it may be quite unrelated to religion. Some would refer, rightly, to the decrees of God's wisdom but see only that side of providence which works in favour of themselves. "It was providential that I took the plane I did because if I had taken the other one it would have crashed." It was just as providential for the people on the other plane. The point is that providence is not something to be invoked on particular occasions and only as affecting one's own affairs for good or ill. It should be seen as the unfolding of God's overall will to which one adapts oneself more and more as the prayer life reveals both its universal and particular application. Thus when it is said in scripture that such and such an event took place "that the word of God might be fulfilled" or "as prophecy had foretold" the first impression is in a way cheating and that the event was foreordained, that it had to fit in with the programme laid down. No escape. But in fact there was every escape, and had an escape been chosen it would itself have been allowed for by the providence of God. Events which take place "as fore-told by the words of prophecy" have God's seal upon them precisely because they were not escaped from when they could have been, and because they fulfilled what God had antecedently willed. The events had fallen out as they had because they had been in conformity with the grace of God.

In conclusion, providence does not exist to intervene when human affairs have got out of hand. It is not just for emergencies. We do not take out a policy in committing ourselves to divine providence, insuring ourselves against loss. God's providence, says St. Augustine, is man's firmament. All that man does is done under its cover. It governs universal things such as the movement of the planets in their courses, and even dull things such as the deliberations of the prices and incomes board, the department of supply and produc-tivity, the local council and its elections. More intimately, it plays a part in the composition of a letter and the bathing of a baby. The more comprehensive a view we can get of God's providence the better. It should incline us to adapt ourselves in his name to the existing order.

9

Adapting Life to Death

The recommendation about how to deal with poachers might apply equally to the subject of death: since we cannot beat death we would be wise to cooperate with it. By looking back too much at the past and clinging to a fear of death we stiffen as we grow older. "From the middle of life onwards" wrote Jung, "only he remains vitally alive who is ready to die . . . for in the secret hour of life's midday the parabola is reversed and death is born. We grant goal and purpose to the ascent of life, why not to the descent?" Carl Jung lived until he was eighty-five, seeing in old age an opportunity of continuous development. Philosophers and theologians join with psychologists in repeating this doctrine but the vast majority of mankind prefer to believe that the less you think about death the better. Here is another psychologist, Erik Erickson: "Any span of the cycle lived without vigorous meaning, at the beginning, in the middle, or at the end, endangers the sense of life and the meaning of death."

Experience would seem to show moreover that those who have made the adjustment early on are the ones who make what is charmingly called the best deaths. They have got used to the idea and the edge of alarm has worn off. Alarm in fact has been replaced by welcome.

Coming to terms with death is one of the surest signs of maturity. And it is also of spirituality. The brave people are those who face danger even though they do not know from what quarter it is coming. Death is not a danger about which we have no knowledge; it is a certainty of which we have no experience. But because it is a certainty we have at least enough knowledge of it to enable us to meet it head on. It would be much worse if we had never been told about death and had not the least idea about what to expect. We are not expected to be brave about it; we are, however, expected to be sensible. Jesus, since he entered into the minds of all men and experienced the fears of all men, was afraid to die. Those who fear death have Christ for precedent.

To think of death more as a leaving than as an arriving may be natural to most people but it is nevertheless to put the emphasis on the less significant aspect. "There is only one journey in which we attain our ideal of going away and coming home at the same time" wrote Michael Kettle, a poet, shortly before he was killed during the First War, "and that is death."

Death is not a chance event, a moment of dissolution, a necessary happening on which there is no going back; it is a law, a habit which differs from the habit of life in that it lasts for good. Looked at from the right end of the telescope, life is a protracted process of dying which meets an appropriate climax before starting off again at an altogether happier level.

"On earth the broken arcs" wrote Browning, "in heaven the perfect round." It is an error of valuation to wish we could go on for ever wheeling a cartload of broken arcs when there is a perfect round to be looked forward to. Writing to the Corinthians, St. Paul might almost be commenting on Browning's lines, and Browning on his. "If there are gifts of prophecy the time must come when it will fail. For our knowledge is imperfect and our prophesying is imperfect. But once perfection comes, all imperfect things will disappear . . . now we are seeing a dim reflection in a mirror; but then we shall be seeing face to face."

Life; death; life again. How can there be any choice? "No eye has seen nor ear heard, nor has it entered into the mind of man, what great things God has prepared for those who love him." And again: "In this present state we groan as we wait with longing to put on our heavenly home . . . we groan and find it a burden, being still in this tent . . . this is the purpose for which God made us, to put the second garment over it and to have what must die be taken up into life, and he has given us the pledge of the spirit." Many of us find that as we grow older we groan a good deal more than we used to. Perhaps we are victims of self-pity, perhaps of impatience, perhaps of disenchantment. An old lady who in her youth had been known for having covered great distances on foot was asked by a newspaper reporter whether she thought walking had contributed to her longevity. (It was her ninetieth birthday.) "I don't think it did" she replied, "because I gave it up a long time ago." "Wasn't that rather a pity?" the reporter observed. "Not really. You see I found that all the miles kept collecting at the end."

After the age of about fifty the years start collecting at the wrong end. It is only then that one begins to notice how long they take. They are like sad old empty envelopes pitched from a dustbin upon the black waters of a slow stream. The full years were earlier on, when the envelopes were addressed. Just a matter, now, of waiting and not making a fuss. But it is worth remembering that this is as important a time as any that has gone before. These are years of testing. More boring, of course; but more fruitful because more secret.

How often do we not hear of old men being tiresome? Would they be tiresome if they pondered more upon the afterlife? Had they schooled themselves in their youth to the thought of a non-menacing death they would probably be less querulous in their old age. People who have spiritual securities to support them are seldom tiresome and exacting: nothing can offer greater secruity than the thought of dying and going to God. "Ah, but what if you die and you don't go to God? What if you believe in him all right but do not die in a state of grace?" Yes indeed, there is just that. Granted that there is all the more need to keep on living as you should in ethical terms, there is also all the more need to trust. Given trust in God's mercy, nothing is impossible. Absolutely nothing. The mistake is to think of the next life as the opposite shore to which we must swim with a weight round our necks. "What if the weight is too heavy before we start?" Nothing is too heavy if we trust. Christ has carried the weight and all we have to do is to dive in when he wants us to and follow the course which he himself has taken. "But the opposite shore is unknown territory; at least while I am on this side I know where I am and have more or less got used to it." Once again it is a question of trust. Those who stand shivering on the bank make things worse for themselves, wanting to know what they are in for and knowing that it does no good to guess. The thought of dying is not meant to be a hideous anxiety. It should be an invitation, an incentive.

Another mistaken approach is to look upon the martyrs with pity. They should be looked upon with envy. If a man cannot die for what he believes he cannot live for what he believes. If we lived more according to our beliefs we would not feel sorry for those who are called upon to put those beliefs to the test. Belief, whether died for or lived for, is the qualifying factor. Belief is even more important than the cause which is believed in. The cause may be doomed to failure, may be mistaken at the outset, but believing in the cause cannot go unrewarded. In our case, which is the Christian ideal, the cause and belief in the cause coincide. The word "faith" covers the two. So, given faith, the question of death is no more and no less disturbing than the question of life. But this is a proposition to which many would give assent but which few find satisfying.

At a less elevated level — and we must take whatever help we can get on this subject — it is worth noting that when people come to die they do not in fact feel the dread which has been a dark shadow to them when in the full enjoyment of life. As the faculties begin to fail there seems to be less in the temporal order to excite the sense of longing. A new norm is substituted for the old and it seems natural rather than abnormal to die. When one is in health this cannot well be imagined but when dying (such seems to be the experience) the perspectives are so altered as to make the possession of health seem remote and less real than the existing condition. Whether by a natural or supernatural dispensation the partings are accordingly eased. People who have any sense of the spiritual at all are confident that eventually they will be reunited with those from whom they are now separating, and against the interruption of human love every other letting go is as nothing. A life's work left unfinished? A place or an environment to be sacrificed? These things do not seem important any more.

Man cannot turn his back forever upon what he knows. He knows about death. It is a reality, and a reality for him. If he follows up what he knows, the subject of death will mushroom into a happiness. If he tries to smother the thought, it will shrink into a fear. Death is not a secret to be buried, sunk deep under a slab of concrete with pretty little rose-trees planted all round it to make people think it can be ignored. Death is the flowering moment of life, and needs no disguising or artificial decoration. Since it is the one vital moment in life which it is important to get right, people pay astonishingly little time ensuring against getting it wrong.

10

Life in Relation to Heaven

One of the things which prevents our getting heaven into focus is the way the human memory works. John Le Carre makes one of his characters say: "We've got the big memory and the small memory. The small memory is to remember the small things and the big memory is to forget the big ones." Of heaven, anyway, this is profoundly true. We treasure so many snapshot recollections of the trivial past (which stand, often quite incorrectly, for a state of happiness which we think we can return to in retrospect) that the big things of life, the afterlife being one of them, are pushed into the background.

People have a good enough excuse for steering away from the thought of death; there is no good excuse for avoiding the thought of heaven. Indeed, as we shall see in a minute, the thought of heaven comes naturally, and is much more of a background consideration in their lives than they realize.

By forming the wrong concept of death, seeing it only as an evil, they form the wrong concept of heaven. They are right in viewing the two in unison, wrong in letting heaven take its colour from the false view of death. The result is that because they want to run away from the thought of death they want to run away almost as much from the thought of heaven. This is memory's fault, not instinct's. Always the backward glance in preference to looking forward. By going over the past and digging themselves in to what was real at the time but is not actual any more, people are wasting their chances of looking forward to the reality of heaven. Heaven is as actual as today, and goes on being actual when today is one of the "small things" which will be remembered imperfectly at best and at worst misleadingly.

In the foregoing chapter the not very original idea of leaving one shore for another was touched upon. We do not prepare ourselves for an inevitable landing by retreating deep into the hinterland which lies at the back of us. We prepare ourselves by studying whatever the geographers can tell us of the country we are facing. Admittedly they cannot tell us much, but it is absurd to shut our eyes to its existence. It is still more childish to ban the mention of bridges and boats. By that freakish tendency which recurs so often in human thinking as to make one wonder whether the freakish is not perhaps the normal, heaven is treated as something so remote as to be almost unreal. To give consideration to heaven is felt to be unrealistic. In fact it would be difficult to think of anything more real than heaven. Heaven is not remote but actual. Heaven is eternal life, and Christ has said that "this is eternal life, to know the Father". This *is*, not this will be but actually *is*.

Man instinctively looks for heaven, and he cannot forever deny himself his instinct. Whenever he looks for happiness —

and philosophers as well as theologians tell us he cannot *not* look for happiness — he looks for heaven. He may not know as much about heaven as he knows about death (he has seen people in death and has not seen people in heaven) but he knows, unless he is a complete fool, that nothing short of heaven can satisfy him. This knowledge, however elementary, must make him happier in the thought of heaven than in the thought of death. Death is a means only, heaven is an end. Death is an event, heaven is an eternity. Death is something which man connects with pain, uncertainty, regret, darkness. He can imagine death in a variety of guises, one of which may conceivably turn out to be true, but however he tries to imagine heaven he knows he must be wrong. This is because memory is no use to him here. So if he thinks at all about heaven it is more with the imagination than with anything else. Far better if he thought about it with his reason.

To picture heaven is as idle as it would be for a mole to imagine what it would be like to be a seagull. Compare heaven with this present life and the best you can do is compare plastic flowers with real ones, the old fashioned magic lantern with cinemascope, shadows with substance. Even to think of it as joy without regret, as love without jealousy, as service without misunderstanding, as peace without boredom, as rest without restlessness, does not get us far. These are only negative concepts, taking the flaws out of such goods as we have been able to experience in life. It is like imagining a watch which will never go fast or slow and will tell the time without having to be wound up. It is like the drunkard thinking of drink without the consequences.

But this has by no means exhausted the ways of thinking about heaven. There is till scripture and there is still reason. St. Paul to the Colossians: "Seek the things which are above, where Christ sits at the right hand of God." In seeking Christ we seek the place he has prepared for us. He who is "the resurrection and the life" gives us, even in anticipation, a share of his heavenly condition. In his letter to the Hebrews St. Paul compared "the things which can be moved", that is the things of this earthly creation, with those that cannot be moved. "Wherefore we have received this kingdom which cannot be moved" where we "may serve God acceptably." We are already citizens, already co-heirs, and all we have to do is to wait. The exile is temporary, and is not at all the same as extradition.

In case this is preaching to the converted, is quoting texts to those who know them by heart and who live by them, there is always the proposition that if there is no heaven then life here on earth is utterly pointless. Can life reasonably be as inconclusive? No questions answered, no appetites satisfied, and love coming to a dead end. If there is no heaven, then this life is a joke in very bad taste.

There is a story which perhaps gives a better idea of heaven to our finite minds than imagination, reason, and theology can manage between them. It is about a Jewish child who had a dream which he felt reluctantly obliged to describe to the saintly rabbi who was responsible for his religious education. "I was granted in my dream" the boy related, "without being seen, to see the blessed as they sat in the court of heaven. Then the Lord came to the place where I was hidden and invited me to pass before each of the holy ones in turn and to note their state of blessedness which would prove helpful to me when I returned to earth." "And what did you observe, my son?" the rabbi asked. "O my master" the boy confessed with evident compunction, "I was deeply disappointed. There was no singing, and if harps there were I did not see them. The angels too, with their eyes shut and their wings folded, were not as I had expected. Saints and angels alike: it was hard to believe they were in heaven at all. What is the meaning of this message, O my master, which the Lord wished to bring home to my soul?" "Perhaps it was that you should know" said the holy rabbi to his disciple, "not that the blessed ones were in heaven but that heaven was in them."

St. Augustine makes the same point when he says that while we naturally look forward to the possession of the plenitude of bliss we do better to think of the plenitude of bliss possessing us. So long as we look forward to being able to give glory to God for all eternity, it cannot matter much. We impose a limitation upon our forward looking if we think only of the eternal happiness which God gives to us.

Epilogue

When Odysseus came to the conclusion (belatedly enough) that it was time for him to leave Circe's island and go home, an interesting conversation took place between the hero and the goddess. (It is in the tenth book of the Odyssey if anyone should want to look it up.) He was right, of course, in deciding to go for he had already stopped on too long — having fathered a child by his hostess, and there had been all that business about the pigs — but the complications which he had now to face were formidable. What he chiefly disliked was Circe's insistence that he take in Hades on the way. He invented difficulties. Standing before Circe he was not so much the brave sailor as the snivelling ex-lover exaggerating the drawbacks of the voyage; he had no pilot, he did not know the way, it was the wrong season for sailing, barnacles had collected on the craft. This is where Circe shows her wisdom. "Odysseus of many stratagems, son of Laertes, progeny of Zeus" she said to him, prefacing her remarks with flattery, "trouble not thyself but be of good heart: hoist thy sail, weigh anchor, and trust the gods." In other words he was to let the divinely ordered seas and the winds take him where he had to go. The gods were not asleep. What he, Odysseus, had to do at this stage was to sit down and not argue or get excited. The island interlude had served its purpose and lasted long enough: it must not be dragged on for there were other adventures to face. Preparations made, plans must not be altered for fear of the future or dread of parting. Above all, the gods must not be told their business. Let Odysseus, in effect, be sensible and take the strong, straight course . . . and not be silly any more.